CW00956901

QUIRK BOOKS
PHILADELPHIA

# CSI:
## CRIME SCENE INVESTIGATION

BY SAM STALL

### THE INTERACTIVE MYSTERY

BASED ON THE HIT CBS TELEVISION SERIES • CREATED BY ANTHONY E. ZUIKER

# MURDERS THE MURDERS TH

© 2009 CBS Broadcasting Inc. and Entertainment AB Funding LLC. All Rights Reserved. CSI: CRIME SCENE INVESTIGATION in USA is a trademark of CBS Broadcasting Inc. and outside USA is a trademark of Entertainment AB Funding LLC. CBS and the CBS Eye Design TM CBS Broadcasting Inc.

CSI: CRIME SCENE INVESTIGATION produced by CBS Productions, a business unit of CBS Broadcasting Inc. in association with Jerry Bruckheimer Television.
Created by Anthony E. Zuiker
Executive Producers: Jerry Bruckheimer, Carol Mendelsohn, Anthony E. Zuiker, Ann Donahue, Naren Shankar, Cynthia Chvatal, William Petersen, Jonathan Littman

Page design copyright © 2009 Quirk Productions, Inc.

No part of this book may be reproduced in any form without written permission from the publisher.

Library of Congress Cataloging in Publication Number: 2009926681

ISBN: 978-1-59474-406-8

Printed in China

Typeset in TradeGothic and Eurostyle

Designed by Doogie Horner
Cover Photograph by Michael E. Reali
Photos on pages 1, 5, 8–10, 13, 15, 61–63, 65, and 72 by Michael E. Reali
Photos on pages 12 and 18 courtesy istock photo
Production management by John J. McGurk

Models: John Kensil (Mel Bledsoe), Nicole Melchiorre (Charlotte Bledsoe), Valerie Temple (Drew Lazaran), John Taggart (cop), Paul Perry and Joe McCarthy (crime scene investigators)

Crime scene locations provided by Dana Spain, with assistance from Maryellen Cammisa and Michael Waxman of Plumer and Associates, Inc., Realtors.

Architectural blueprint designed by Julie Scott.

Distributed in North America by Chronicle Books
680 Second Street
San Francisco, CA 94107

10 9 8 7 6 5 4 3 2 1

Quirk Books
215 Church Street
Philadelphia, PA 19106
www.irreference.com
www.quirkbooks.com

"What a crime."

CSI GRAVEYARD SHIFT
SUPERVISOR Gil Grissom
glanced over at the speaker.
It was field investigator
Nick Stokes. Hearing such
a frank statement of the
obvious piqued his
curiosity.

As did the fact that Stokes was staring intently at the ceiling.

"Well . . . yes," Grissom said. "It's definitely a crime. That's why we're all here."

The two other people in the room, Las Vegas Police Department captain Jim Brass and assistant coroner David Phillips, nodded.

Stokes kept looking up.

"I was talking about that," he said, pointing toward a corner. "See where the crown molding joins? It's slightly uneven. Uneven. In a house this expensive, that's a crime."

Grissom glanced at the living room's woodwork.

"Good eye," he said. "But let's focus on the crime on the floor rather than the one on the ceiling. I think it's the bigger deal."

He looked down at the fifth member of their group: Melvin R. Bledsoe, until recently a well-known developer of high-end Las Vegas–area residential communities.

Now Bledsoe lay on the floor, slowly cooling to room temperature. Yet even in death he was still every inch a VIP. Were it not for him, the bulk of the LVPD's CSI team wouldn't be combing his house at 1:00 on a Monday morning. And Gil Grissom and his associates wouldn't be puzzling over what—or, more accurately, who—put him in such straits.

The case began at 11:08 p.m. when the Las Vegas Police Department received a terse 911 call. It came from a private security guard named Mitch Harding who was patrolling the neighborhood.

"Shots fired at 1021 Mountain Air Court," he

shouted. "The guy's still in the house. Get out here now."

Despite the timely warning, the police arrived too late to do anything but secure the area and wait for the CSIs.

"Tell me what we know so far," Grissom said.

Phillips knelt beside the body. It lay face-down on what had formerly been a very expensive antique Indo-Persian rug. Nearby, ID tents marked the locations of a broken glass and a fireplace poker.

"He grabbed the poker from the fireplace in his bedroom," Stokes said. "A weapon of opportunity. Not very helpful in a gunfight."

"He's been dead about two hours," Phillips offered. "That jibes pretty well with the 911 call."

The assistant coroner had left the body in place while he photographed it from every conceivable angle.

"Ready to roll him over?" Stokes asked.

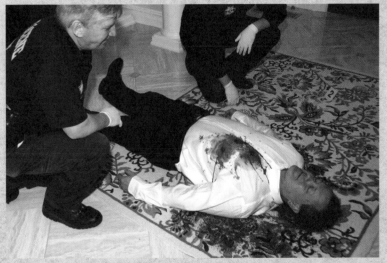

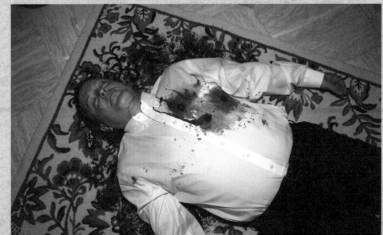

"Yeah," Phillips said. "Please grab his legs."

Grissom watched as Phillips and Stokes turned the corpse face-up. It took a moment to rock it free of the viscous, red-black blood adhering it to the rug's dense pile.

Stokes let out a low whistle. "Anybody got any theories about the cause of death?"

It was a joke. The cause was obvious—a trio of blue-black holes perforating the front of Bledsoe's expensive dress shirt.

"Pretty good shooting," Brass said.

"Or just luck," Grissom said. "The killer surprised Bledsoe and fired at nearly point-blank range. Where did he enter the house?"

"First-floor utility room just off the kitchen," Brass said. "He left that way, too. Busted the window to unlock it."

"Where did he go after that?"

"We figure he got in and out by scaling the wall surrounding the development. It's quite a piece of work—ten feet tall, with a network of motion sensors on the interior side. In theory, anyone who got over the thing would be instantly detected."

"In theory," Grissom said. "So why wasn't our intruder?"

"We're checking. I'll get back to you when I have an answer."

Grissom stared down at the corpse. "What's in his pants pocket?"

It looked like a small pamphlet. Phillips photographed the discovery in situ before carefully extracting it.

"It's some kind of booklet," he said. "Got some blood spatter on the cover, but I can make out the title. *Gardens of Serenity: An Anthology of Classic Japanese Haiku.*"

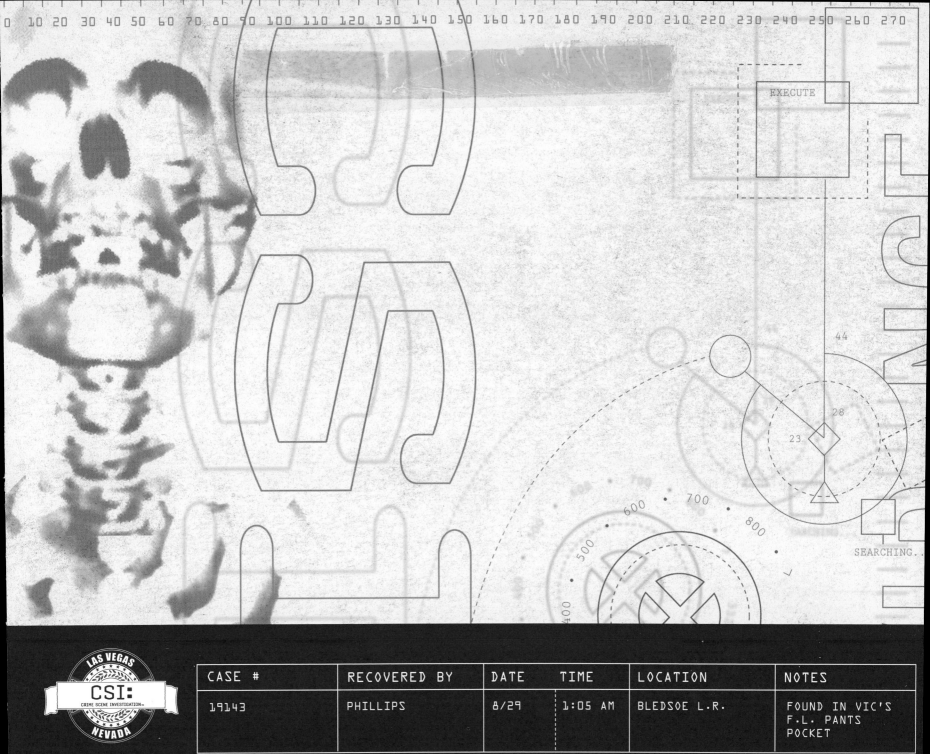

LAS VEGAS  CSI: CRIME SCENE INVESTIGATION  NEVADA

| CASE # | RECOVERED BY | DATE | TIME | LOCATION | NOTES |
|---|---|---|---|---|---|
| 19143 | PHILLIPS | 8/29 | 1:05 AM | BLEDSOE L.R. | FOUND IN VIC'S F.L. PANTS POCKET |

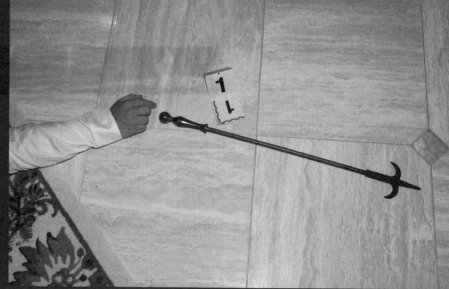

"Interesting," Grissom said. "Definitely not the sort of thing I'd expect this guy to tote around."

Phillips passed the book to Stokes, who placed it in a plastic evidence bag.

"Haiku is Japanese poetry, right?" Brass asked.

Grissom nodded. "Each poem is only three lines long. In English there are five syllables on lines one and three, and seven on line two. The point is to get as much meaning into as little space as possible."

"Books are fun to read / but useless in a gunfight / try running instead," Brass said, counting off the syllables on his fingers.

"Very nice," said Grissom. "You should use that at your next poetry reading."

"So our shooter broke the window to get in," Stokes said. "Bledsoe came downstairs. They met here, in the living room. The shooter came around *this* corner, and his victim around *this* corner. They confronted each other. The intruder had a

gun, Bledsoe had a fireplace poker and his poetry book. Bam, bam, bam."

"The end," Grissom offered.

"Not quite," Stokes responded. "There's little bits of landscaping mulch going all the way up the stairs. Same stuff in the planting bed outside the utility room. After he gunned this guy down, the gunman stepped right over him and kept going."

"Show me where he went," Grissom said.

Brass and Stokes led the way up the elegant hardwood staircase to the second-floor landing. But Grissom didn't really need the guidance. His trained eye followed the subtle trail of organic matter right into the home's master suite.

He took a moment to survey his surroundings.

"Very eclectic," Grissom said as he took in the four-poster bed, fireplace, a seating area full of overstuffed furniture, and, in the farthest corner of the immense space, an ornate desk with a mirror-shiny top that looked big enough to land an airplane on.

"Well, at least the molding was installed correctly up here," Stokes said as he once again examined the trim work. "Otherwise it's a nightmare. Nothing in here makes sense, design-wise. All it says is, 'I've got money, so let's spend it.'"

"I didn't know you were an interior design expert," Grissom said. "Remind me never to have you over to my place."

"Get a load of the bed," Brass said.

A large oil painting in a gold frame lay in the middle of the luxurious-looking bedding.

"I assume that's not where it belongs," Grissom replied.

"You assume correctly," Brass said. "It was found there, probably tossed aside so the killer could get at this." He motioned toward an alcove out of direct sight from the doorway. It contained a wall safe—open and empty.

Grissom took a closer look. About a foot wide, a foot deep, and perhaps eighteen inches tall, it contained nothing but air. "How'd the killer open it?"

"Either he had the combination or he cracked it himself," Brass said. "I'm guessing that, given his short stay, he had the combination."

"What was the lag between the 911 call and the first officers on the scene?" Stokes asked.

"No more than ten minutes," Brass said.

"So, Bledsoe came downstairs when he heard the noise of the utility room window breaking?" Stokes continued. "That seems strange. The master suite's a long way from there. It doesn't seem like the sound would make it that far."

Grissom surveyed the room. Something on the faraway desk caught his eye. He walked over to it. "Bledsoe was work-

ing here," he said, mostly to himself.

He examined the surface, which betrayed an almost obsessive orderliness. No personal papers of any kind were visible. No candy wrappers, no stray paperclips, no dust. There was just one oddity: a large flat-screen monitor with a blizzard of sticky notes surrounding the screen. Each contained a phone number, an address, or some other bit of data hurriedly scribbled in what Grissom assumed was Bledsoe's handwriting.

The only other sign of disarray was an iPod seemingly tossed aside. It perched precariously on the left side of the desk, just as the police had found it.

"He didn't 'hear' anything," Grissom said. "He was wearing this iPod when it happened. Everything on this desk, in this house, betrays an orderly mind. Bledsoe wouldn't have just tossed this iPod on his desk unless he'd been in a hurry."

"The desk chair's still right where we found it," Brass offered. "About four feet away from the desk, like he kicked it or something to push it out of his way. Which he probably did, because he didn't have to hear the guy breaking in. Chances are he saw it."

"How?" Grissom asked.

"On this," Brass said, pointing to the darkened monitor. "The entire house is rigged with video cameras."

"You mean the interior?" Grissom asked.

"Interior and exterior. They're all wired into a couple of monitors. One in the kitchen and one here. Bledsoe could have watched the break-in live, as it happened."

"Oh my God, please tell me all those cameras were recording," Stokes said.

"Yes and no," Brass replied.

"I sense this isn't going to be good," Grissom said.

Brass sighed and shook his head. "The system is very sophisticated. The cameras dump everything onto a central hard drive, creating a visual record of whatever happens in the house."

"Creepy, but potentially very helpful," Grissom said. "However, the fact that you don't seem the least bit excited by this concerns me."

Brass sighed again. "Storing visuals from twelve wireless cameras takes up a lot of space on the hard drive. Too much, it turns out."

"Here it comes," Stokes said.

"Even if you had unlimited memory, there's no need to store useless footage. So every four hours, unless it's told to do otherwise, the system dumps everything, wipes the hard drive, and starts over."

"Great," Stokes said. "When did it do its last wipe?"

"About two hours ago," Brass continued. "Just after the murder and just before we arrived."

"So there's nothing of use?" Stokes said.

"Nada. The living room camera is on the ceiling, providing a God's eye view of everything that happens. We have some nice footage of the body lying on the floor, and of the LVPD responding. Then Bledsoe's wife showed up and, a few minutes later, someone from his office. Then we shut the system down ourselves. Archie Johnson took the CPU back to the lab. Maybe he can salvage something. But he wasn't optimistic."

"Neither am I," Grissom said. "Was there an alarm system?"

"A good one. All integrated into the monitors. The minute it went off, all dumping protocols would have been overridden and the system would have taped until it ran out of memory. The video files would also have been automatically transferred off-site via a wireless Internet connection, just in case some clever crook destroyed the in-house hardware to cover his tracks."

"Ingenious," Grissom said.

"Ingenious, but not fool-proof," Brass said. "None of these things happened because the victim forgot, or never intended, to arm the system. If it hadn't been for the 911

call, this guy would still be lying on the floor, waiting for his wife to get home."

"Have you spoken to Mrs. Bledsoe?" asked Grissom.

"Not much. She'd just returned from a spa weekend in Scottsdale. She was standing at the airport baggage claim when we called, and then she came straight to the house. We had a man on the front door but she pushed her way past him."

"So she's got a solid alibi," Stokes said.

"Yeah," Grissom added. "But the timing of her trip is interesting. Anyone else come around?"

"No one who can help us, if that's what you mean," Brass said. "Shortly after Bledsoe's wife left, we had another visitor—a woman named Drew Lazaran. She was Mel Bledsoe's administrative assistant."

"How did she get word of this?" Stokes asked.

"LVPD contacted her right after the killing was discovered. We needed a phone number for Mrs. Bledsoe. But apparently whoever spoke with her refused to explain why we wanted the digits. Just said something cryptic about there being a family emergency. Lazaran said she stopped by the house to see if she could help."

"Did you speak to her?" Grissom said.

"Yeah, briefly. When she saw what had happened, she became agitated almost to the point of incoherency. Really chewing on the scenery."

"Not everybody looks at murder victims for a living. What did you make of her?"

"Attractive. Smart. Good mistress material. But that's just between you and me and the dead guy downstairs."

"Where is she now?" Stokes asked.

"I cut her loose. I told her we'd be in touch."

"Fine. Anything else?"

"I'll let you know if the kid who phoned in the murder says something interesting. I'm on my way out front to see him now."

Stokes, Brass, and Grissom walked back downstairs to the living room where the body lay. The small crowd that had formerly filled the room—taking photos, dusting for fingerprints, collecting samples—was thinning out. The easy part—finding things—was over. The tough part—putting it all together—was about to begin.

"Good hunting," Grissom said to Brass. "Anything else we should know about Mr. Bledsoe?"

As if on cue, a gurney was rolled in for the corpse.

"Tell you more after the autopsy," Phillips said. "But I'd say, from the entry wounds, that we're looking at standard nine-millimeter pistol ammo fired at close range."

"Keep us posted," Grissom said. "Judging from the number of news trucks out front when we arrived, our rich friend will be the lead story on the news this morning."

· · · · · · · · · · · · · · · · · · · · · · · · · · · ·

Brass made his goodbyes and exited Mel and Charlotte Bledsoe's palatial home—an imposing, six-thousand-square-foot mansion equipped with swimming pool, six-car garage, and tennis court. When he'd first arrived, the security person at the development's front gate had given him directions to the place. She told him to

keep an eye peeled for a "Spanish colonial."

But to Brass the monstrosity didn't seem worthy of such a stately name. To him it looked like the unholy offspring of a basketball arena and a Taco Bell.

Of course, it wasn't all that different from the other sprawls of brick and mortar he'd passed on the way in. They were all part of an exclusive community that, seven years earlier, had been just another patch of parched scrubland on the Vegas periphery. Now it boasted a golf course, two clubhouses, and pretty much every other frill one would associate with the highest of high-end living. The name of the place, Passion Lake Preserve, said it all.

But the gates and the cameras and the private security couldn't defeat human nature. Even here, in the lap of luxury, you could still wind up shot dead on your living room floor.

"Some passion," Brass muttered. "Some preserve."

The kid he needed to talk to was Mitch Harding, one of Passion Lake Preserve's finest. He was part of the cadre of

security guards charged with keeping this little corner of Upper Crust Heaven safe.

Brass found the lanky twenty-five-year-old sitting on the bumper of his private patrol car, smoking a cigarette. His uniform seemed to sag on his spare frame. To Brass's practiced eye, he looked authentically rattled.

The detective introduced himself and got down to business. "So, what did you see?"

Harding took a long drag on his cigarette. "I was driving through the development, making a routine circuit," he said. "You can ask my boss. This is what I do every night about this time. Just a slow, random pass. Show the residents we're on the job."

"I understand," Brass said. "So when you got to the Bledsoe house, what did you see that looked—"

"Suspicious? I saw there were a couple of lights on upstairs and that the downstairs was dark. And then I saw three quick bursts of light through one of the downstairs windows. I knew they were muzzle flashes."

"How'd you know?" Brass asked.

The kid shrugged. "I guess I saw it in a movie."

He tossed away the butt of his cigarette, fished a crumpled pack out of his breast pocket, tapped out another, and lit it. Brass noticed that the kid's hands shook.

Harding noticed that he noticed.

"Sorry," he said. "When I get nervous I smoke."

"Feel free," the detective said. "So, you saw the flashes and called 911. Then you drove back to your office. I'm thinking that procedure would probably have dictated that you call in, then at the very least wait here for the police to arrive.

Maybe you could have seen the guy leaving the house and gotten a description."

"Only if I'd had night vision goggles," Harding said. "Look around you. It's pitch black out here. That guy could have run right past me and I wouldn't have spotted him."

"Well, I assume you have a flashlight. And your car has a spotlight. You could have—"

"I freaked, all right?" Harding said, a bit louder than necessary. "I totally freaked. I'm just not prepared for this sort of thing. Who goes to work every day expecting to deal with this kind of crap?"

"You'd be surprised," Brass said. "So you saw the flashes and you dialed the police. What happened then?"

"I called my supervisor and I left. I drove back to the office to report in, and when I heard you guys needed to talk to me, I came back." Brass looked at him, expecting more, and Harding shrugged. "Look, I've only got twelve hours of training. Two hours of practice with my sidearm. They're paying me minimum wage. I figured I'd get out of the way and let the grownups take care of this."

"It's okay," Brass said. "You couldn't have helped the victim anyway."

Just at that moment the corpse of Mel Bledsoe, swathed in a large black body bag and strapped to a gurney, was wheeled out the home's front door and past Brass and Harding on its way to the coroner's van. Harding watched it trundle by, then dropped his cigarette, ground it out with his left foot, and placed his head in his hands.

"I'm not cut out for this crap," he said. "I'm going to be a home theater installer. I'm taking the classes right now. No shootings, no cop stuff. Just a nine-to-five gig. Can I go?"

"Sure," Brass said. "Just don't go far."

The kids head suddenly snapped up.

"Why not?" he asked. "All I did was call it in."

"I'm just saying that we might want to ask you some more questions. So don't go wiring any out-of-state home theaters, okay?"

"No problem," Harding said. "If you need me, I'll be around."

Probably curled up in the fetal position somewhere, Brass thought. "One last thing," he said aloud. "Where were you parked when you placed the call?"

"Right over there," the kid said, pointing to the far side of the driveway.

As Harding's car pulled away, Brass looked down at the two cigarette butts the kid had left behind. He noted the brand. Then he pulled out a clear plastic evidence bag and gathered them up.

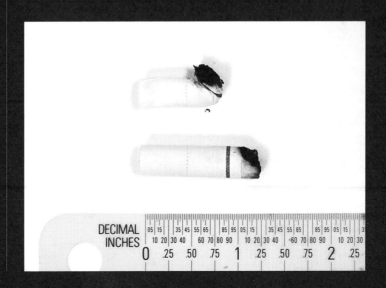

pon returning to the CSI offices, Grissom's first order of business, even before asking about Bledsoe's autopsy, was to see if specialist AV technician Archie Johnson salvaged anything from the home monitoring system's hard drive.

He found the equipment, a nondescript black box, squatting on Johnson's cluttered desk. It was hooked up to a large, high-resolution monitor not too different from the one at Bledsoe's house.

Grissom could tell by the expression on the tech's face that the news wasn't good.

"There's nothing," Johnson said. "The files weren't just deleted, they were electronically shredded. Very thorough work."

"Why would they bother?" Grissom said.

"Privacy. This system was everywhere in the house. Anyone with access would know everything about you. Would you want footage of yourself getting dressed, or arguing with your spouse, or kicking the dog, preserved forever on a computer hard drive?"

"Guess not," Grissom said. "But then I wouldn't have a system like this in the first place."

"Yeah," Johnson said. "Creepy."

Grissom studied several small, isolated images pushed to the left side of the screen.

"Screen grabs," Johnson said. "I figured I'd save a shot of everybody who showed up after the killing."

PATROLMAN // 11:25PM

CSI // 11:35PM

CSI // 11:37PM

CHARLOTTE BLEDSOE // 12:28AM

CHARLOTTE BLEDSOE // 12:27AM

DREW LAZARAN // 12:40AM

CHARLOTTE BLEDSOE // 12:45AM

DREW LAZARAN // 12:43AM

"You do that," Grissom said. "Let me know if you find anything else."

"Trust me, I won't," Johnson said dejectedly.

Grissom returned to his office, sat down heavily behind his desk, and surveyed his surroundings. Every inch of available space had a piece of arcane ephemera perched on it. There were jars containing preserved animal specimens. A mounted tarantula bigger than a grown man's hand. And butterflies, carefully arranged in a glass case.

Some of his associates thought this place was a cluttered mess. But Grissom knew it wasn't. If you understood the system, he mused, it all made sense. What looked superficially like chaos was really order, though an order that obeyed its own peculiar protocols. You just had to figure out what they were.

It was the same with a crime scene. Chaos on the surface.

But if you looked carefully, gathered enough information, tried to see through the eyes of the person who committed the crime—divined their motives, even their emotional state—one could understand. What looked like a jumble of pieces could be assembled into a clear picture.

Right now, he knew, the Bledsoe killing was at the "jumble of pieces" stage. And, frankly, he could use a few more pieces. Plus a little less public interest in the case.

His phone rang. When he picked it up, the person on the other end didn't bother to identify himself. He just started talking.

"The press is calling these guys 'The McMansion Murderers,'" the voice said.

"That's actually pretty good," Grissom replied. "Though personally I would have preferred 'The Cul-de-Sac Killers.' It's

got just the right mix of whimsy and menace."

"You said, 'killers,'" the voice stated. "So it was more than one guy?"

"I don't know. We believe only one person entered the house, but there could have been an accomplice, or accomplices, outside. The actual shooter probably ran to the development's perimeter fence about 200 yards away, climbed it, and escaped by car."

Grissom glanced at his watch. It was a bit past 3 a.m. He tried to imagine the person on the other end of the line—none other than LVPD Sheriff Rory Atwater—pacing back and forth in his bathrobe, glancing up periodically at the early, early news on his TV.

"The press is all over this," the sheriff said. "Bledsoe was a big name. So is his wife. She does a lot of that big-time charity crap. She's got friends at city hall. A couple of them have already called me, asking what the hell's going on. So what the hell is going on?"

"We're working on it," Grissom said.

"Which means you don't have anything yet," Atwater said.

"We're working on it," Grissom repeated.

"Work faster," Atwater replied.

The conversation ended the way most such "motivational" chats did. The sheriff told Grissom to move mountains and expedite matters because this was a high-profile case, the entire city was watching, and so on. Then Grissom reminded his superior that he and his people were doing their best, just as they did with all their cases. He also reminded him that Bledsoe's wasn't the only killing in Las Vegas.

It wasn't even the only killing in that evening.

Shortly after he hung up with the sheriff, Catherine Willows entered his office. To Grissom, she seemed to smell slightly of charred toast.

"Want to hear about Burn Guy?" she asked.

Grissom pushed the Bledsoe case temporarily aside. "Burn Guy," as Willows called him, was a corpse found in an incinerated house in a low-rent neighborhood in the unincorporated town of Paradise. Its boundaries included everything from a large section of the Strip to bustling McCarran International Airport to sprawling neighborhoods both well-to-do and grindingly poor.

Mr. Burning Bed died in one of the latter.

The call for CSI assistance with that case had arrived at pretty much the same moment as the Bledsoe alert. Because they were shorthanded, Willows, in what Grissom considered a sterling example of team play, went out solo to process the scene. It was the sort of selflessness not just anyone—especially someone like Willows, who held the rank of CSI supervisor—could be expected to show.

"Lay it on me," Grissom said.

Willows sat down and opened a folder.

"The victim is tentatively identified as the home's occupant, Mateo Espinoza, age twenty-eight. Found face-down on his bed, shot once in the back of the head at close range. The house was partially burned, probably intentionally. Preliminary fire department reports indicate use of an accelerant in the bedroom where the body was found. It was some sort of commercial lighter fluid. I could smell it when I arrived."

"Anything of interest in the house?"

"Not superficially. All I can say, based on the parts that

didn't burn, is that the fire was probably an improvement. Mr. Espinoza wasn't exactly rolling in cash. No real furniture except for the bed. And the yard was full of junk. Cinder blocks. Trash bags. Broken glass."

"We can't all be rich real-estate developers," Grissom mused. "Did anyone see or hear anything?"

"No witnesses so far," Willows said.

"Figures. It's been that kind of night. Anything else?"

"Autopsy is pending. But here's something interesting we found at the scene."

Willows handed Grissom a color, 8-by-10 inch crime scene photo. He had to study it for a moment before he understood what he was seeing. In the middle was a large, finely cut diamond. It was surrounded by charred flesh.

"Is this Espinoza?" Grissom asked.

"Yes," Willows confirmed. "Specifically, the upper-left quadrant of his torso."

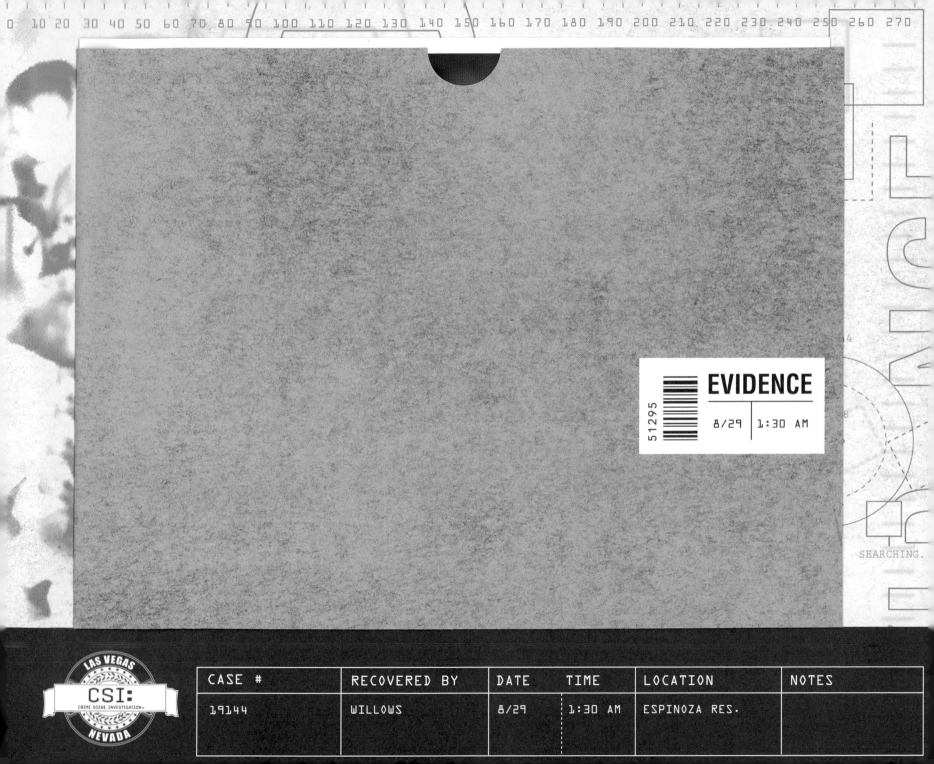

0 10 20 30 40 50 60 70 80 90 100 110 120 130 140 150 160 170 180 190 200 210 220 230 240 250 260 270

**EVIDENCE**

51295

8/29 | 1:30 AM

SEARCHING.

LAS VEGAS
CSI:
CRIME SCENE INVESTIGATION™
NEVADA

| CASE # | RECOVERED BY | DATE | TIME | LOCATION | NOTES |
|---|---|---|---|---|---|
| 19144 | WILLOWS | 8/29 | 1:30 AM | ESPINOZA RES. | |

Grissom picked up a magnifying glass and studied the image.

"Is this part of a nipple piercing?" he asked.

"That's what the location suggests. There appears to have been some kind of mounting associated with it, which the heat of the fire severely deformed. I can tell you more once it's removed from the body and examined."

"Did you find the murder weapon?"

"It wasn't at the scene."

"Any leads? Any theories?"

"Nothing right now. All I can say is that somebody shot him in the back of the head and then torched the place."

"Not very subtle."

"Well, not every case can be a high-profile mystery involving a well-known captain of industry."

Grissom smiled. "True enough," he said. "Just remember that, in pretty much every way that matters, these cases are the same."

"Pardon?" Willows said.

"In life they were different. One was rich and well known, the other poor and obscure. But that changed tonight. Now they're both exactly the same—corpses in morgue lockers, rapidly cooling to 55 degrees Fahrenheit. They could be lying right next to each other right now, for all we know."

"The equality of death," Willows said, playing along.

"Exactly. And now it's up to us to find out what brought them to this."

Willows rubbed her forehead.

"I got a headache while I was out at the scene," she said. "The house is in the landing approach for McCarran, and the

noise from the jets overhead was incredible. This philosophical stuff isn't easing my pain."

Grissom smiled.

"Well, thanks for taking one for the team. And please keep me informed."

Willows smiled back and rose to leave. "Keep *me* informed," she said.

Alone again, Grissom thought for a moment more about the two cases. Actually, they were different in one important way. While a lot of people clamored to know what had happened to Bledsoe, so far no one had even inquired about Espinoza. No family, no friends, no nothing.

So perhaps, even in death, some people were more equal than others.

. . . . . . . . . . . . . . . . . . . . . . . . . . . . .

As if to confirm this very thought, Brass stopped by a few minutes later. He knocked on the frame of the door to get Grissom's attention.

"Any news?" Grissom asked.

"Only bad. Remember those motion sensors that are supposed to detect anyone who might have jumped the wall around Passion Lake Preserve?"

"Of course. Let me guess: The system was deactivated."

"No, it was working just fine. But according to the development's chief of security, it works a little too well. They get approximately thirty to forty hits every night. The 'intruders' are anything from coyotes to rabbits to residents out walking around. There's no way to differentiate a potentially dangerous contact from all that background noise, so . . . "

". . . so they ignore everything."

"Correct. However, the computer that oversees the system logs every blip. It shows that the sensor on the stretch of wall nearest to the Bledsoes' home was activated at 10:52 p.m. So that's likely when the killer hauled his sorry butt onto the property."

"Wonderful," Grissom said. "Anything of interest at the wall itself? I don't suppose this guy would have done us the favor of dropping his wallet."

Brass smiled. "We found the spot where he entered. All we have is some footprints on the exterior side, where he walked through the hardpan on his way to the wall. He wore a deep-treaded work boot, size twelve. On the interior side there's a spot where the grass is beaten down. Seems too big for just footprints. It looks like he maybe lost his footing and landed hard."

"Do we have any idea how he made it over the wall?"

Grissom asked.

"Superficial scratch marks on the masonry indicate some sort of grapple. He hauled himself up on a rope, tossed the grapple down onto the far side, then tossed it up there again when it was time to leave."

"And then what?"

"There's an isolated two-lane road only ten yards from the wall. Considering the time of night, he could have just parked on the asphalt—or, more likely, had an accomplice wait there with a car. Really, getting over the wall was the tough part. The rest was cake."

"Wonderful," Grissom said.

"I have more less-than-good news. Charlotte Bledsoe is here. Says she wants to talk to someone about the investigation."

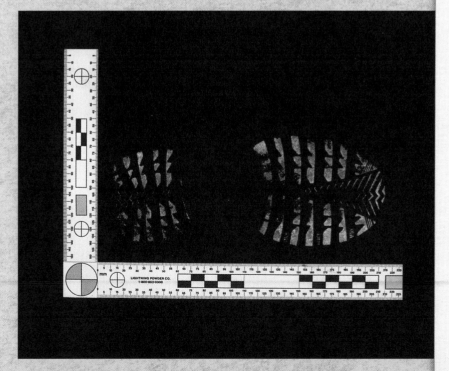

Grissom glanced at his watch. "It's four in the morning."

"She probably went to a hotel someplace, then started thinking about what happened. I'll bet it's just now starting to sink in."

"Of course. Where did you put her?"

"Well, I certainly wouldn't think of bringing her in here," Brass said, his eyes landing on Grissom's collection of animal specimens preserved in alcohol-filled jars. "The woman's had enough shocks for one night. She's in my office. You want to join me?"

"Yes. We'll tell her what we know, and maybe she can tell *us* a few things, too."

. . . . . . . . . . . . . . . . . . . . . . . . . . . . . . . . . . .

Brass's workspace was as well ordered as Grissom's was chaotic. The detective sat behind his desk. Grissom and Bledsoe sat in front of it. The two men offered their condolences.

Charlotte Bledsoe reminded Grissom of those well-dressed, well-heeled women who were forever wandering into the offices of 1940s private detectives, desperately in need of help. She appeared remarkably alert and awake for a woman meeting law enforcement officers at four in the morning. Her dark hair was stylishly done, but a bit unkempt—understandable, given the circumstances. She wore a camel-colored suit that looked like it cost more than Grissom made in a year.

"My husband didn't deserve this," Bledsoe began. "He didn't deserve to be murdered in his own living room by some—some random idiot."

Brass noted her clothing. She'd changed from the casual dress he recalled her wearing when he saw her briefly at the house. Perhaps she wanted to present herself as a woman who meant business.

"So you think the attack was random?" he asked. "No one had a vendetta against your husband?"

"Oh, there were plenty of people angry with my husband. But none of them would do something like this. We don't move in those kinds of social circles."

Grissom and Brass glanced at each other.

"Mrs. Bledsoe, since you're here, perhaps you could assist us with a couple of things," Brass said. "The man who killed your husband also opened a wall safe in the master suite. Do you know what it contained?"

"A few of my husband's papers, but also the bulk of my jewelry collection. Our insurance company appraised it for half a million dollars."

Motive established, Grissom thought.

"That's a very nice collection," he said aloud. "Why didn't you keep it at a bank or someplace more secure?"

"I said the same thing to my husband on several occasions. But he didn't want to put something that valuable under the care of others. He was . . . . I guess you could say he was paranoid about things like that. Anything that was important to him, he tended to watch very, very closely. You've seen our home security system."

"It's pretty extensive," Brass said. "Most people wouldn't be comfortable with that level of scrutiny."

"I wasn't comfortable with it," Bledsoe said. "But Mel wouldn't budge on the issue. He was extremely concerned about safety."

"Then why didn't he arm the home security system?" Brass asked. "You'd think, given his mindset, that it would be very important to him."

"Mel had a great deal of trouble remembering the proper codes. He tended not to bother with it when we were actually home. He once said that if someone broke in while he was around, the alarm system would be the least of their worries."

A cloud of grief passed briefly over Bledsoe's features. Her mouth crumpled for a moment. Then the anger returned.

"If he'd gone with me this weekend, none of this would have happened," she said. "The house would have been robbed, but he would be alive."

"You went away to a spa," Grissom said. "He was supposed to go, too?"

"Yes," Bledsoe said. "It's a place called High Desert Retreat, just outside Scottsdale. They have a two-day stress-relieving regimen. Deep massage therapy and such. I talked him into going."

"Things pretty stressful at work?" Brass asked.

"Of course. My husband specializes in top-of-the-line luxury home construction. The market for his product isn't what it used to be."

"So why didn't he go to the spa?" Brass asked.

"I was packing on Friday afternoon when he called from the office. Something very important had come up and he needed to stay in town," Bledsoe said. "I asked him if it was really that pressing. Mel tends to think lots of things are very, very important. But he was adamant. So I went without him."

"Did he tell you what it was?" Grissom asked.

"No. It could have been any number of things. Ever since the market tanked, he's been involved in one legal dispute after another. Several of his subcontractors have sued him for breach of contract. He's sued a couple of people, too. You can't imagine how hard this downturn has been on the housing industry. There are a lot of hard feelings. A lot of desperation."

"Any of those individuals seem particularly desperate?" Brass said.

Bledsoe instantly caught his meaning.

"As I said, we don't move in those kinds of circles," she sniffed. "Plus, these people have financial problems that wouldn't be solved by doing this."

"Has anything strange or unusual happened in your lives recently?" Grissom said.

Bledsoe thought for a moment.

"There is one thing," she said. "Mel mentioned that the problem he was working on was a 'security issue.' I assumed he was talking about his office. But he might have meant the break-ins."

Grissom and Brass's eyebrows shot up simultaneously.

"What break-ins?" Brass asked.

"Over the last year there have been two other robberies at Passion Lake Preserve," Bledsoe explained. "Nobody got hurt, but it drove Mel absolutely insane. That whole place was built around the idea of being safe. Those thugs were turning him into a liar. It was becoming embarrassing."

Brass, as discreetly as possible, started tapping on his computer keyboard.

"When did these robberies take place?" Grissom asked.

"One about a year ago, another maybe six months later. Like I said, no one was hurt. No one was even home at the time. The robbers didn't bother with big things like TVs. They took cash, jewelry—"

Bledsoe suddenly stopped talking. Through a fog of grief, anger, and fatigue, she glimpsed the outlines of something terrible.

"It was them," she said. "They killed my husband."

"We're considering every possibility," Grissom said. "Right now, at this stage, we're not excluding anything."

Bledsoe didn't seem to hear. "Could they have targeted him? Because he was trying to stop them?"

"Perhaps. But we have many, many leads to pursue before I'd be comfortable offering a theory. I'll be keeping you in the loop, of course."

"Me, too," Brass said. He was now staring intently at something on his computer screen. "And thank you for coming in. As my associate said, we'll keep you posted of any developments. We may be in touch if we have further questions."

Bledsoe stiffened. "That's it? Shouldn't you ask if *I* have any further questions? I didn't come out here in the middle of the night so I could listen to platitudes and then get shoved out the door."

"I'm sorry to be so brusque," Grissom said, "but whoever did this to your husband is still out there. The quicker we get back to the case, the quicker we can catch him. I'm sure you understand."

That seemed to mollify her. For the moment, at least. Bledsoe departed reluctantly, with a promise to check in later. She was almost out the door when Grissom stopped her.

"One other thing," he said. "Your husband was carrying a book of Japanese poetry when he was killed. Do you have any idea why?"

Bledsoe shrugged. "He found it a few months ago and he's been carrying it ever since. He once told me the poems gave him insights into his life and his relationships, but they never gave him any peace."

"I don't understand," Brass said.

"Neither did I," Bledsoe said. "I think he somewhat enjoyed the fact that I didn't grasp what he said. If you figure out what he meant, I'd like to know."

With that she departed.

"She could be as big a problem as the press," Brass said.

"She's got a right," Grissom said. "So, what about those break-ins? I assume that's what you were hunting up on your computer."

"Yeah. The first was on May 10 of last year, the second on October 21. Both were Passion Lake homes. The MOs were identical: Someone entered via a first-floor window while the occupants were away, stole only high-value, easily transportable items, and left."

"Were the houses tossed?" Grissom asked.

"You mean, did these guys spend much time looking around? No. The reports say that except for the broken windows that were used to gain entrance, there wasn't a thing out of place. But here's the really interesting part. The big-ticket item taken during the first robbery was a collection of jewelry. It came from a safe in the basement that was hidden behind a false wall. Whoever took it knew exactly where it was."

"Inside job," Grissom said. "Come morning, I'd like someone to talk to the neighborhood's head of security. I'm sure they've got sign-in/sign-out sheets for the day of the killing. We'll need to talk to every single one of those people. Maybe something will shake loose."

CAPT. JAMES BRASS

"So what about Charlotte Bledsoe's theory?" Brass asked. "Do you think there's any chance he was intentionally targeted?"

"No, not at all. These guys go to a great deal of trouble to avoid that sort of thing. They want money, not hassles. They ran into Bledsoe by accident and panicked. That is, if they actually did this."

"You doubt it?"

Grissom sighed. "Well, at the moment it's definitely our most promising lead. But there's something about it . . . . "

"I know," Brass said. "I'm always a little put off when someone involved in the case waltzes in with a neat, ready-made theory."

"Yeah," Grissom said. "It makes me wonder about that story—and about the person who gave it to us."

. . . . . . . . . . . . . . . . . . . . . . . . . . . . . .

Thanks to Grissom and Brass's conversation a few hours earlier, LVPD detective Samuel Vega found himself standing, bright and early, inside the main guardhouse at Passion Lake Preserve. He noted that, besides a set of ornate-but-functional gates, the main entrance was equipped with formidable-looking retractable spike strips. He half-expected to see the concrete barricades used at military bases.

The developer—Bledsoe—had also piled a series of artfully constructed hills around the perimeter, to prevent prying eyes from getting an easy look at the opulence within. And to keep the masses from intruding on what the develop-ment's brochures described as "the most luxurious, relaxing atmosphere in either Las Vegas or its environs," the entire 170-acre complex was ringed by a forbidding security wall. Vega couldn't begin to imagine how much it must have cost.

"I wonder if they planted land mines," he muttered under his breath.

"Excuse me?" said the uniformed security guard in front of him. Her name was Shauna Hart. She looked to be thirty-five, with blonde hair tied in a ponytail.

"Nothing," replied Vega.

She resumed rummaging through a large, leather-bound log book.

"Here's yesterday," she said, handing over a large sheet of paper. "The day before is on the other side."

As Vega surveyed the sign-in/sign-out sheet, his stomach started to churn. There were twenty-one names on the front of the page, and another twenty on the back.

EVIDENCE

51495

8/29 | 8:12 AM

ARCHING...

LAS VEGAS
CSI:
CRIME SCENE INVESTIGATION™
NEVADA

| CASE # | RECOVERED BY | DATE | TIME | LOCATION | NOTES |
|---|---|---|---|---|---|
| 19143 | VEGA | 8/29 | 8:12 AM | PASSION LAKE MAIN GUARD HOUSE | |

"So, how many security people does it take to hold down the fort here?" he asked.

"Three on the day shift, three on the night shift," Hart said.

"Forgive me for asking, but what do you guys do?"

"Staff the two entrances. Drive around. Show the flag."

"Any calls?"

"For assistance? Occasionally. We helped a lady locate her Visla the other day."

"A Visla? Is that a car?"

"A Hungarian hunting dog. It got out when a housekeeper left the backdoor to her employer's pool house open."

"Sounds exciting."

Hart's expression soured.

"Look, don't give me a hard time," she said. "I've got a criminal justice degree and spent five years with the San Diego police department. The only difference between you and me is that I got shot in the right knee during a convenience store robbery. Physically I can't make the cut on a real police force anymore. I try to console myself with the fact that I don't have to risk having my head blown off to get my paycheck."

"Point taken," Vega said. "Speaking of earning your money, has anyone on your staff seen anything unusual lately? Maybe the same car driving by the entrances a little too slowly or a little too often? Someone lurking where they shouldn't be?"

"This is a gated, patrolled neighborhood," Hart replied. "Nobody lurks. If you're a guest, someone has to let you in. If you're here to mow the lawn or to shampoo a rug or to walk somebody's dog, you sign in and out. Twenty-four hours a day,

seven days a week, 365 days a year."

"Well, with all due respect to you and your staff, somebody got in. And your boss is dead because of it."

Hart's face pinked slightly. "Point taken. I'll ask around."

"I may, too, after I finish with these lists."

"I have contact info for most of them. The housekeeping people, the landscaping guys. And you can probably corner a lot of them here on the property, while they're working. We'll get you names and numbers."

"I'd appreciate that," Vega said.

He got into his car and proceeded to perform a small errand for Brass. Noting the time, he turned over the engine and headed deeper into Passion Lake Preserve. Obeying all posted speed limits and stop signs, he drove to Mel Bledsoe's home. He stopped in front of the driveway, once more noted the time, and did a little quick math.

It took about one minute, twenty-one seconds to go from the guard house to the Bledsoe residence. Vega dialed Brass on his cell phone, gave him the figure, and hung up.

•  •  •  •  •  •  •  •  •  •  •  •  •  •  •  •  •  •  •  •  •  •  •  •  •  •  •

Across town, Nick Stokes sat down with Lou Todman, owner of United Confidence—the installer of Bledsoe's monitoring system. Todman's office was immaculate. The man himself was somewhere in his fifties, with gray, carefully trimmed hair. He wore a dark blue suit, complete with vest.

"So, does something like this hurt business?" Stokes asked.

"Not really," he replied. "The system wasn't on, so it can't be blamed."

"That sort of thing happen often?"

"More than you'd think. You don't have to be an electronics genius to get around this stuff. You just have to be lucky. People get tired of fooling with the keypads, or they just forget. So these monster electronic watchdogs are often fast asleep. Bledsoe, I think, was a particular problem. He just couldn't seem to remember the codes for arming and disarming the system."

"Were your systems installed in either of the other two Passion Lake houses that were robbed?"

Todman grimaced.

"Both of them," he said. "But statistically that's not too strange. I've worked on two-thirds of the home in that development."

"Were either of the systems active when the robberies took place?"

"Nope. In both cases the residents went out someplace for the evening. Maybe they were running late and didn't want to bother. Their surroundings probably lulled them into a false sense of security. I mean, that place is called Passion Lake Preserve. It certainly sounds safe, doesn't it?"

Stokes smiled.

"Don't believe everything you hear," he said. "So, tell me about the monitoring system."

"There were twelve cameras, eight in the house and four outdoors," Todman said. "All wireless, all very small. All were linked to two in-house monitors. From either location, you can get full-screen views of any one of the monitors, any two, or split-screen views of all of them at once."

"Wow," Stokes said. "That's a lot of cameras. Is that . . . "

"Unusual? Yes, but it's becoming less so all the time. In Passion Lake I've put monitors in fifteen houses. There was a rush of business after word got around that Mr. Bledsoe had them installed in his house. Of course none of my other clients wanted anything nearly as . . . "

"Intrusive?"

"You said that, not me. I'd prefer the word 'comprehensive.'"

"Okay. So I take it that if the security system and the monitors are both online, there's no way someone could get in undetected."

It was Todman's turn to smile.

"Here's a dirty little secret," he said. "If it's up against your typical spur-of-the-moment home breaker with no training or brains, my gear will win every time. Our sign in the front yard is enough to make a novice think twice. But if you've got a crew with experience and technical savvy, what can I say? Machines are still no match for human ingenuity."

"I see," Stokes said. "So what do *you* use?"

"Me? I've got a nervous, hair-triggered dog that barks at every little thing. She's a better security solution than any electronic gadget on the market. But please keep that information to yourself. I have to make a living."

"Will do," Stokes said. "We've already taken in the CPU, but I'd like to look at the rest of the hardware. Could you supply us with the locations of the cameras at the Bledsoe house so we can collect them?"

"I can save you the trouble," Todman said. "Mrs. Bledsoe

called a few hours ago and said she wanted everything removed, toot sweet. She sounded pretty upset. I tried to explain that the system wasn't armed, and that it didn't fail. But it was no use. She wanted every bit of the security package—I believe she called it 'that goddamned spy network'—out of the house. So we sent someone over there this morning. All the gear should be in the back somewhere."

"I thought you said the system couldn't be blamed," Stokes said.

"Not if you think about it logically," Todman said. "This has nothing to do with logic."

A couple of minutes later Stokes found himself deep inside United Confidence's service area, talking to company tech Kevin Williams. He wore a scruffy beard and a ratty T-shirt that said, inexplicably, "I Make My Own Gravy." Somewhere in his mid-twenties, he seemed the very model of a socially stunted computer nerd.

Williams seemed excited to have a visitor—excited and a bit agitated.

"There you go," he said, pointing to a cardboard box on a nearby worktable. "Those are the cameras. Brought them in a little while ago. The two monitors are in my office."

"How long did it take you to rip this stuff out?" Stokes asked. The fact that everything had been taken from its original context and extensively handled irritated him. Granted, the odds of finding anything useful amongst this junk had been thin from the start, but now the chance was vanishingly small. Stokes wondered if it was worth the trouble to lug the box to his vehicle.

"Easy come, easy go," Williams said, just a touch too exu-

berantly. "Everything's wireless, so there's no ripping. The toughest part is finding all the cameras, then climbing up a ladder and grabbing them."

"Finding them? Don't you have a schematic or something?"

"Oh, yeah," Williams said, glancing around his cluttered work area. "But it's still a pain."

Stokes rummaged through the box of cameras. There were two kinds—an almost impossibly miniscule model for interior use and a sturdier, slightly larger version for outdoors. The outside cameras looked a touch weather-beaten.

"The inside cameras are small, but not as small as we could make them," Williams volunteered. "There are 'snake-eye' units that could be completely concealed inside, say, the pattern of a wall treatment. But that would require some pretty intrusive wiring. And to be frank, those teeny, teeny cameras kind of freak out the clientele. Makes them feel like they're living in the Big Brother house. Know what I mean?"

Stokes ignored the rambling remarks. "Is this all of them?"

"Yeah," Williams said.

"I'll get them back to you when we're finished. I'm going to need that schematic, too, so I'll know where the cameras were positioned."

"Not a problem," Williams said, and he retrieved a large folded document from his workstation.

DRYWALLING **ACE** SERVICES

# F A S T .   E F F I C I E N T .   B O N D E D .

## ACE DRYWALLING SERVICES

handles any size job, from basement remodeling to fire or flood restoration to industrial and commercial. Family owned since 1972, you can expect topnotch service from our employees.

Ask about our special rates!

### WE ALSO DO:
- Trimwork
- Door hanging
- Window replacement
- No job is too la    mall!
- Ask about our     ounts for customer re

Office Hours: 8 a.m.-6     -6 p.m. S

How to Contact Us:     ur website  at ww

LAS VEGA
CSI
CRIME SCENE INVESTIG
NEVADA

EVIDENCE
51495
8/29 | 1:45 AM

When Stokes knocked on Grissom's door, he almost welcomed the change of subject. "Any news?"

"I just came from United Confidence," Stokes explained, placing a small surveillance camera on the desk for Grissom's inspection. "This is a piece of the gear that Kevin Williams says he removed from the Bledsoe residence. It's a weatherproof camera for exterior use. But there's a problem. All of the outdoor models were somewhat weather-beaten, but this one's wear pattern is different from the others. Not as pronounced."

"Could it be a replacement?" Grissom asked. "Perhaps it wasn't in place as long as the others."

"I don't think so. There's roofing tar on the mount, but the Bledsoe's home has a tiled roof. Plus the serial number is squirrelly. The other outdoor units all come from the same production batch. This one's entirely different."

Brass appeared in Grissom's doorway, holding two plastic evidence bags containing cigarette butts; he had heard enough of their conversation to leap right in. "Maybe one of the Bledsoe cameras malfunctioned," he offered. "They could have just grabbed a used one out of the backroom to replace it. You should talk to that Williams guy, see if they have some sort of record."

Stokes smiled. "Oh, I think we need to talk to Williams again, but we might want to do it in an interrogation room."

"What have you got?" Grissom asked.

"Archie and I went out to the Bledsoe place on the off-chance we could find the 'real' camera. We located it near the garage, up against the house behind some roses, where it must have fallen off its mount. The landscapers dumped a huge load of mulch on it. I can understand why Williams, who probably also tried to find it, failed."

"Did it give you anything helpful?" Brass asked.

"We think so. The camera, just like all the others, is wireless. It transmits to the home monitoring system's CPU via radio. In most home security systems, these signals have an effective range of about one hundred feet—just enough to reach the computer and maybe spill out a bit onto the lawn. But Archie says this camera was set to broadcast its signals a quarter mile. If it was a mistake, it was a big one. Anyone with the appropriate equipment could have parked on the street in front of the Bledsoe house and seen what the camera saw. Or any of the other cameras if they were set up the same way. All he'd need is a monitor."

Grissom perked up.

"What was the range on the other cameras?" he asked.

"About one hundred feet, just as they should be," Stokes responded. "But they could have been recalibrated after they were collected. Maybe, just maybe, they were all set on long range before Williams got to them. The only reason we have this one is because he couldn't find it."

"But isn't the broadcast signal encrypted?" Brass asked.

"Yes," Stokes said. "But that wouldn't be a problem if you had the codes. And you know who has the codes?"

"Kevin Williams," Grissom said. "So, he's setting this equipment at maximum range, then using a receiver to look inside the house. He could park on the street and case the place for a robbery."

"But there's just one problem," Brass said. "I've seen the sign-in/sign-out sheets for Passion Lake. Williams hasn't been there recently, except to remove the Bledsoe system."

"I can't imagine him robbing a house, anyway," Stokes said. "He doesn't have the stones for that kind of work."

"Let's bring him in for a chat," Grissom said.

"Actually, let's reserve both interrogation rooms," Brass said. Grissom and Stokes looked at him.

"I think I know who did the actual dirty work," he said, holding out the evidence bags he had brought to the meeting. "If we get them both in here at the same time, we can close this investigation."

. . . . . . . . . . . . . . . . . . . . . . . . . . . . . . . . . .

An hour later Williams found himself in the smaller of CSI headquarters' two interrogation rooms, seated alone at an austere metal table.

Stokes, along with Grissom and Brass, observed him through the room's two-way mirror. They watched as the tech's right foot tapped out a nervous staccato beat on the cold, naked floor.

"I'm going in with you," Brass said. "I'll stay until our other guest arrives."

"The more, the merrier," replied Stokes.

Williams nearly jumped out of his skin when Stokes and Brass walked into the room. They left the door open.

"I thought it was time we met at my place," Stokes said. "Do you recognize this?"

He plunked the camera he'd found down on the table. It landed with a forbidding clank. Williams couldn't take his eyes off it.

"It's from the Bledsoe house?" Williams replied.

"Yep. But it's not one of the twelve you boxed up and gave to me. One of those was a plant. So I went back to locate the real one. I found it, and I discovered something really curious."

"What?" Williams said.

"You already know. I'll give you one chance to tell us yourself."

Williams swallowed. Tiny beads of perspiration collected on his forehead. "This could get me fired," he whispered.

"Right now that's the least of your worries," Brass retorted.

Williams glanced at Brass, then at Stokes. "Like I told you before, old lady Bledsoe wanted everything removed, rush, rush," he said. "I drove out there and started pulling stuff. I tracked down eleven, but it took longer than I planned. And then I spent forever hunting for the last one. Bledsoe started looking at me funny, so I gave up and split. I figured maybe I'd come back sometime and try again. But then you showed up and I panicked. I just tossed an old camera from another job in the box, figuring you wouldn't notice. Only now I realize my mistake. I forgot to check it off the blueprint."

"So that's it?" Stokes said.

"What do you mean?" Williams said.

"Is there anything else you'd like to share? About the camera itself?"

Williams looked like a cornered animal.

"I—I don't know what you mean," he stammered.

At that moment a uniformed officer stepped briefly into the room and made eye contact with Brass, who nodded in reply.

"I've got to go," he said. "Our other guest has arrived."

Williams watched him walk out.

"What's happening?" he asked Stokes.

"Look for yourself," he said, nodding toward the hallway.

At that moment a very concerned-looking Mitch Harding, lately of the Passion Lake security force, walked past, escorted by Brass. He and Williams briefly made eye contact.

The look of shock and fear that passed across both their faces told Stokes everything he needed to know. He walked over to the door and closed it.

"So here's what happens next," he said. "You and your buddy are going to have a race. He'll sit down in the next room and tell his story while you tell yours in here. The person who's most truthful and helpful enjoys some leniency during charging and sentencing. The person who's least helpful finds himself in more trouble than he's already in. Which is quite a bit. So I'll ask again—is there anything you'd like to share?"

In the other interrogation room, Brass got down to business as well. He began by showing Harding the plastic evidence bag containing the two cigarette butts.

"Your brand," he said. "We found it on the street, just a little bit down from the Bledsoe residence. Right where you said you spotted the muzzle flashes. You told us you were passing through on a patrol, but you actually stopped—stopped long enough to smoke these down and toss them out the window."

Harding looked at the evidence bag with the same combination of fear and horror that Williams had betrayed upon see-ing the "lost" camera.

"I phoned it in," he said desperately. "I'm the one who called 911."

"Yes, you certainly are," Brass replied. "It's impressive that you spotted those muzzle flashes from so far away, and even more amazing that you knew what they were. It's almost unbelievable."

Brass picked up the bag with the cigarette butts, looked at it, and set it down.

"So what were you really doing out there while you smoked these?" he asked. "And what did your buddy in the other room have to do with all of this?"

Harding took a deep, ragged breath and started talking. Next door, Williams did the same.

. . . . . . . . . . . . . . . . . . . . . . . . . . . . .

It took just a few minutes to get the outlines of what happened. Williams and Harding couldn't share their stories fast enough.

"I met him through a course I teach at the community college," Williams said of Harding. "It's about home theater installation. I do security stuff, but putting in those home theaters is my first love. He worked at the same neighborhood where I installed a lot of systems. We came up with a plan."

"I made regular night patrols, which Kevin said was perfect," Harding offered. "He started tuning the wireless cameras he installed so that I could pick up their signals from the street as I drove by. We'd select a house and then I'd make passes over several nights, going from camera to camera, looking

for goodies. Jewelry, cash, anything small and easy to carry."

"Once Mitch gathered enough data about a particular place, we'd strike," Williams said. "We always worked at night, obviously. We learned enough about the residents to know that they didn't arm their alarm systems religiously. We'd wait until we knew they'd be gone."

"Which of you did the actual breaking and entering?" Stokes asked Williams.

"Neither," Williams replied. "That's not in our skill set. Mitch knew a guy. We brought him in, fifty-fifty."

"There are three of you," Stokes said. "How could the deal be fifty-fifty?"

"This guy got fifty percent and we got the other fifty percent. But he took all the real risks. Plus he's kind of scary. We didn't want to piss him off. Besides, what were we going to do, shop around for a burglar?"

"Good point," Stokes said. "So he killed Bledsoe?"

"No!" Williams said. "He wasn't even there. Hell, we weren't even planning a robbery for that night. Couldn't have done it if we'd wanted to."

"Why not?"

"The burglar guy—his name is Harvey something. Mitch said he was locked up for being drunk and disorderly. He's still there now, I think."

At almost the same moment in the room next door, Harding was telling the very same portion of the tale.

"The guy we use, Harvey Keller, is in jail for some drunk and disorderly thing," he told Brass. "I was on a recon mission, working up some business for when he got out."

"So walk me through the time line," Brass said. "You went

out on patrol, then stopped near the Bledsoe house to watch some TV. What did you see?"

"For maybe the first five minutes, nothing. I was toggling from one camera to the next when I spotted some guy dressed all in black break open one of the downstairs windows. I guess I sort of . . . "

"Freaked?" Brass offered.

"Yeah. I freaked. I switched over to the living-room camera just in time to see him shoot Bledsoe. I couldn't believe it. I didn't know what to do. So I called 911 and headed back to the office."

"It took you a long time to get there. Your time sheet says you returned at 11:15 p.m., seven minutes after you placed the call. But I had an associate of mine see how long it takes to travel between the house and your office, and he made it in less than a minute and a half. So where were you?"

"I drove around looking for someplace to ditch the stuff. Nothing seemed very secure. So I pitched it into a retaining pond. Kevin wasn't too happy about that. But it was the best I could do on short notice."

"Really? Are you sure you weren't actually inside the Bledsoe house, killing Mel Bledsoe and then cleaning out his upstairs safe?"

"Oh, no," Harding said dismissively. "I'm not a murder suspect."

Brass raised his eyebrows. "Really? You seem like one from where I'm sitting."

Harding shook his head miserably. Brass figured he'd probably kill for a cigarette at this point.

"Look, I watch TV," the kid said. "I know what those foren-sics people can do. If I'd walked into that place, you'd have fingerprints, shoeprints, residue from my hands and feet that you'd match to the steering wheel and floorboards in my car—on and on. But you didn't find anything like that because there's nothing to find. I'm in the clear."

"Well, maybe for the murder," Brass said. "But I don't think you'll be installing home theaters anytime soon."

"Hey, I phoned it in," Harding said pleadingly. "I could have just driven away, you know."

"Thanks for the tip," Brass said. "I'm sure the judge will take your humanitarian streak into consideration during sentencing."

Harding let out a disgusted sigh.

"I guess it's true," he said. "No good deed goes unpunished."

. . . . . . . . . . . . . . . . . . . . . . . . . . . . . . . . .

While Harding and Williams were processed, Stokes, Brass, and Grissom convened in Brass's office to talk about the Bledsoe murder case. Or, rather, the lack of a Bledsoe murder case.

"Look what Harding had in his wallet," Brass said. "Can you believe the stones on that guy?"

He offered Grissom a sheet of paper. It was some sort of puff piece about the Bledsoes from a local lifestyle magazine called *Vegas Alive!* from three years earlier, before the housing market tanked.

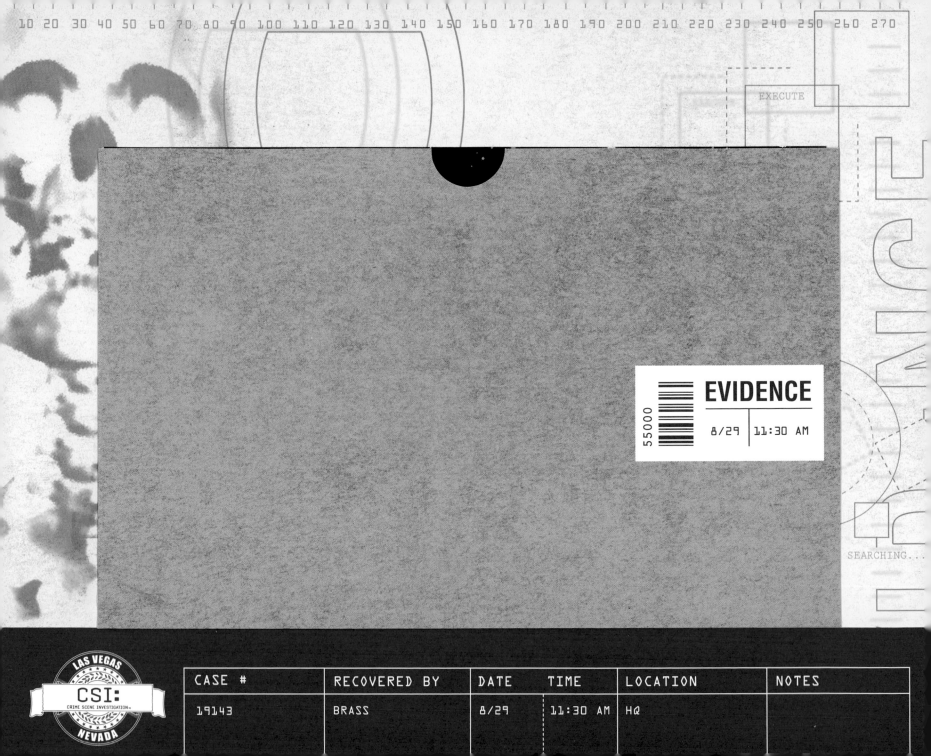

10 20 30 40 50 60 70 80 90 100 110 120 130 140 150 160 170 180 190 200 210 220 230 240 250 260 270

EXECUTE

SEARCHING...

55000 EVIDENCE

8/29 | 11:30 AM

LAS VEGAS

CSI:
CRIME SCENE INVESTIGATION

NEVADA

| CASE # | RECOVERED BY | DATE | TIME | LOCATION | NOTES |
|---|---|---|---|---|---|
| 19143 | BRASS | 8/29 | 11:30 AM | HQ | |

"You've got to love that magazine," Grissom said, handing back the page. "It makes research so much easier. Even two-bit criminals can bone up on their victims."

"Their burglary buddy's out of circulation," Brass said. "He wrecked a car in Reno, resisted arrest, then blew a blood alcohol level of 0.9. He's been in jail for several weeks, including on the night of the robbery. Williams was teaching one of his classes that evening, and Harding—well, we know where he was."

"So they're all in the clear for the shooting," Grissom said. "The McMansion Killers are really just the McMansion Burglars."

"We've spent a long time chasing the wrong guys," Brass said.

His desk phone rang. Brass picked it up.

"Let me take this," he said. "It's Vega out at Passion Lake."

Grissom and Stokes talked while Brass spent about two minutes on the phone. When he hung up, he looked like a new man.

"Vega was interviewing the owner of a company that does drywall work in Passion Lake. He got the name from the sign-in/sign-out sheet. The guy tells Vega that Bledsoe's case is getting too much attention, and he wishes the cops would spend a little time solving the murder of one of his ex-employees."

"And that would be ..." Grissom asked.

"Mateo Espinoza. Remember him?"

"Otherwise known as Burn Guy," Grissom offered.

"Exactly. And you'll never guess where the company did a project a couple of months ago, back when Espinoza was still on the payroll."

"Bledsoe's house?"

"Right again. Burn Guy helped replace some basement drywall."

Suddenly the mood in the room changed.

"Let's go see Catherine," Grissom said.

They found her at her desk, poring over reports from the Espinoza killing.

"What's up?" she said. "You need some assistance with the Bledsoe case?"

Grissom smiled in spite of himself.

"Actually, it seems you've been working on that case, too," he said. "We just didn't realize it." He brought her up to speed.

"Big-time developer mixed up with a small-time hood," Willows said, ruminating. "I don't see the connection. I was just looking over this guy's record. Brushes with the law—most of them involving petty theft—dating back ten years. But nothing to suggest he'd try something of the scale of the Bledsoe robbery."

"Anything high-profile in his record?" Grissom said.

"Not unless you count high-profile stupid. His biggest 'heist,' if you want to call it that, was rifling through some woman's purse while working as a security guard at the Lucky Stakes Casino a year and a half ago. I talked to the chief of security there. He sent over the report."

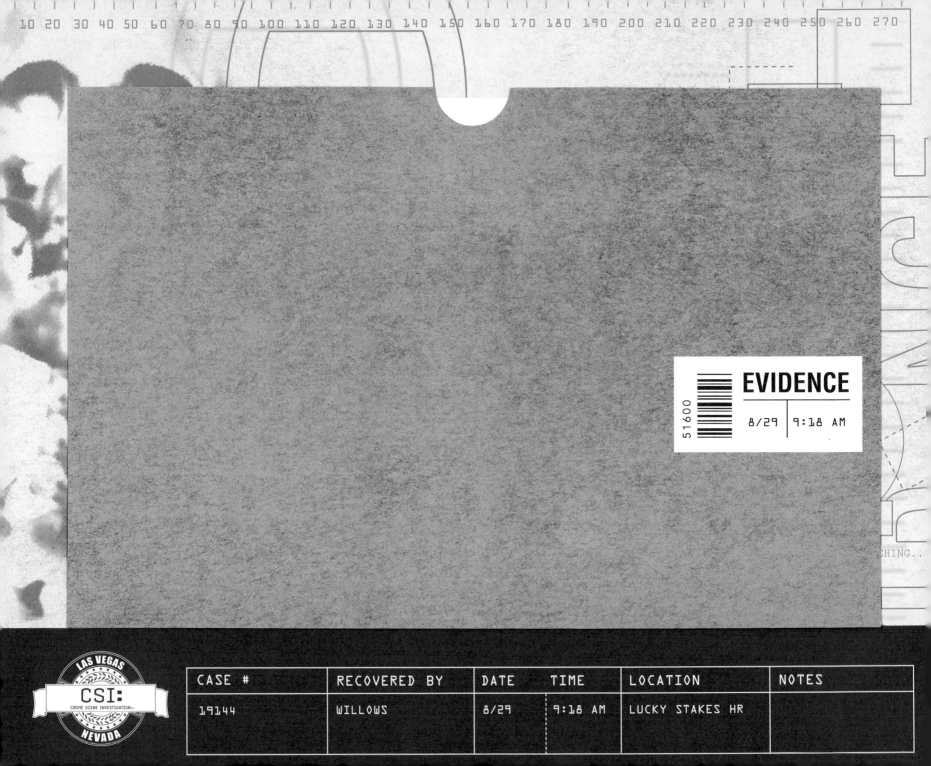

10 20 30 40 50 60 70 80 90 100 110 120 130 140 150 160 170 180 190 200 210 220 230 240 250 260 270

51600

**EVIDENCE**

8/29 | 9:18 AM

CHING...

LAS VEGAS

CSI:
CRIME SCENE INVESTIGATION™

NEVADA

| CASE # | RECOVERED BY | DATE | TIME | LOCATION | NOTES |
|--------|--------------|------|------|----------|-------|
| 19144 | WILLOWS | 8/29 | 9:18 AM | LUCKY STAKES HR | |

"How could he not know that he'd be filmed?" Grissom asked. "Didn't he notice all those cameras overhead?"

"From what I've gathered, Mr. Espinoza wasn't much for brains. But he did get lucky on this occasion. The woman who owned the purse refused to press charges."

"Lucky guy," Grissom said. "We need to get together at your earliest convenience and compare notes."

"I'll pull together everything I've got," she said. "There's a couple of tests pending that might be helpful. I'll see if I can move them along."

"Thanks," Grissom said.

Brass walked into the room.

"Charlotte Bledsoe's on the phone. She wants to speak with you about her husband's case."

"Okay," Grissom said. "I think I have some more questions for her, too."

Grissom took the call in his office. Bledsoe, with minimal preamble, started speaking.

"Mr. Grissom, I've been told by some of my friends that you've arrested three people on charges concerning my husband's death," she said.

"I'm afraid whoever gave you that information was mistaken," Grissom replied. "We've apprehended some individuals involved in the robberies at Passion Lake Preserve. But we do not believe they murdered your husband."

"One of them is a Passion Lake security guard, is that correct?"

Your friends are very well informed, Grissom thought with irritation. And they talk too much.

"I'd prefer not to discuss the specifics of the case right now," he said. "However, we do have another lead that could potentially be very useful. Are you familiar with a Mateo Espinoza?"

Bledsoe seemed to hesitate.

"I don't think so," she said. "Who is he?"

"He did drywall work for the company that remodeled your basement last summer. He quit about two months ago. He was found murdered on the same night as your husband. Do you have any recollection of him?"

Again, the silence on the other end of the line seemed to last a bit too long. Perhaps she was trying to remember the truth. Or formulate a lie.

"I'm afraid I can't help you," she finally said. "I couldn't tell you the first thing about the people who maintain my home, let alone someone who formerly did maintenance on it. Good day, Mr. Grissom. I'll check back later."

Then she hung up.

Which struck Grissom as odd. During their previous encounter she'd been so persistent he'd thought he might have to trigger the building's fire alarm system to escape her. This time, she couldn't wait to get off the line. And there was something in her voice after he told her that Espinoza was dead. Just a bit of a tremble. Maybe she was angry. Maybe it was something else.

Either way, Charlotte Bledsoe suddenly seemed like a far more interesting person.

. . . . . . . . . . . . . . . . . . . . . . . . .

Brass stopped by the offices of Bledsoe Homes on a fishing expedition. He wanted to talk to Mel Bledsoe's assistant, Drew Lazaran.

The company's headquarters occupied one of the upper stories of a glass-swathed high-rise just north of the Strip. The lobby brimmed with contemporary-looking leather furniture, and the walls were painted a shade of light green that had been everywhere a few years back. The receptionist's desk was a brass and blond wood rampart that floated in the middle of the space like a rowboat on a pond.

Behind it on the wall were the words "Bledsoe Homes! We're Building the Future for You!"

It all smacked of irrational exuberance.

Brass figured the view from the lobby, surrounded on two sides by floor-to-ceiling windows, must be spectacular at night. Just now, however, the late-afternoon sun revealed mostly the nondescript rooftops of casinos. It all looked rather tawdry. But then so do a lot of places and things—and people—if you shine a bright enough light on them.

His reverie was interrupted when Lazaran walked into the lobby. Her colorful outfit teased the boundaries of the term "workplace acceptable." Everything on her body—from her flourescent green blouse to her rhinestone pumps—had likely come from a vintage second-hand boutique. Under different circumstances, she might have looked pretty—but today she looked tired and stressed.

"Detective Brass," she said. "Will you come back to my office?"

Brass followed her through the carpeted sanctum of Bledsoe Homes, one of a handful of the cities' high-end developers to survive the housing bust. But that had been before the boss's death. The detective noticed that at least half of the cubicles he passed were empty. Color pictures of the company's past triumphs hung on every bit of available wall space. They were housing developments with names like Golden Mountain Meadows and Roycewood Estates.

Lazaran led him into a small office located next to a much larger one with a closed, locked door. It was, of course, Bledsoe's. LVPD had already gone over the place with tweezers.

The two sat down in a pair of chairs on the far side of Lazaran's desk.

"So, how's business these days?" Brass asked.

"Not good before," Lazaran said. "Worse now."

"Who's running the show?"

"There are several minority partners, but Mr. Bledsoe was the undisputed leader. He was the only reason we kept afloat in this horrible market. Now we've got three people trying to take his place, all while the entire operation sinks beneath them. Just between you and me and the bankruptcy lawyers, I don't think we'll keep the doors open much longer."

Brass looked around her office. There were several filled, sealed cardboard boxes sitting discreetly in one corner. A couple of shelves in the bookcase behind her desk had been emptied.

"Why do you hang around?" Brass said.

"They pay me," Lazaran said. "So far, in all the confusion, no one's realized that a dead man doesn't need a personal assistant. Until they do, I'm happy to let them subsidize the search for my next job."

"What, exactly, did you do for Mr. Bledsoe? Secretarial work?"

Lazaran smiled.

"It was a little more complex than that," she said. "I hold an accounting degree, and I helped him on occasion with the number crunching associated with this business. It wasn't his forte."

"That must have been difficult for him," Brass said. "I understand he liked to play things close to the vest."

"You're absolutely right. But number crunching wasn't his thing. He had to have help, and I gave it to him."

"Then perhaps you could answer some questions about his financial situation. Mrs. Bledsoe said her husband was involved in several lawsuits. Could you elaborate on that?"

"In this field, you're always involved in lawsuits. Just now there are two cases pending against us from subcontractors—people whom we retained to work on various projects. But if you want the details, you'll have to go through our legal counsel. I'm not trying to be evasive. I just don't know the particulars."

"We'll talk to them," Brass said. "Also, did Mr. Bledsoe ever mention a man named Mateo Espinoza?"

Lazaran's eyes grew slightly wider.

"The name's familiar," she said. "Did Mrs. Bledsoe say she knew him?"

"No," Brass said. "Should she?"

Lazaran got up, closed the door to her office and returned to her desk.

"If she doesn't remember him, then he must not have been very good in bed," she said. "They had an affair."

"Says who?"

"Said Mr. Bledsoe. He seemed to know all about it."

Brass sat back in his chair, taking a moment to process the discovery. He'd conducted hundreds, perhaps thousands, of these so-called fishing expeditions over the course of his career. The key was to have low expectations. Most people want to help, but they just don't know anything. So you cast your line and it comes up empty, again and again.

But now here he was, reeling in a catch of a lifetime. It was immediately suspicious. "How do you know about this?" Brass asked.

"Mr. Bledsoe mentioned it once—and only once. I think he'd just found out. He seemed very, very rattled by it."

"How so?"

"Because he didn't share details of his private life. Not ever. But one day I walked into his office and found him staring at his laptop computer. He'd gone completely white. I asked what was wrong, and he said he'd caught his wife having an affair. I asked him when, and he said, 'Just now.'"

"What did he mean by that?"

"He said he had Internet access to the monitoring system in his house. Occasionally he'd log on and go from camera to camera. This time he said he happened to catch his wife doing the drywall guy in one of the upstairs bedrooms."

"What else did he say?"

"Nothing. That was it. I think if I'd come in five minutes later, after he'd had a chance to gather himself, he wouldn't have mentioned it at all. He was that kind of person. Kept things to himself."

"What did you say?"

"What could I say? I just sat there with a dumb look on my face. Later we both pretended it never happened. He never spoke of it again."

"Mrs. Bledsoe said that her husband was supposed to accompany her last weekend on a trip, but that he canceled at the last moment. Did he say why?"

"Not to me. But I do remember seeing a copy of their prenuptial agreement in his briefcase. I have no idea why he'd want that, unless . . . "

"Unless what?"

"Charlotte was Mr. Bledsoe's third wife, so I'm sure he had a very tight agreement. Maybe he wanted to look it over before . . . "

"Serving her with divorce papers?" Brass asked.

"You said it, not me," Lazaran responded.

"Had he told her he wanted a divorce?"

"I don't know. Except for the spy camera incident, which was mostly a matter of my being in the wrong place at the wrong time, I usually wasn't privy to what he did after hours. Unless . . . "

A thoughtful look crossed her face.

"Unless he told her just before the trip," she offered. "Maybe that's why they didn't go away together. That would make sense, wouldn't it?"

Brass regarded Lazaran appraisingly for a moment. He let her words hang in the air for a second or two longer than seemed comfortable.

"Perfect sense," he finally said. "Thank you for your time."

ater, at CSI headquarters, Brass joined with Grissom, Willows, Stokes, and Vega. They tried to put their two cases together.

"Your chat with Lazaran proved helpful," Willows said.

Brass nodded. "She gave us the soap-opera angle between Charlotte Bledsoe and Mateo Espinoza. And she also, by accident, revealed that she's got a gambling problem."

Grissom perked up. "How so?"

Brass produced an evidence bag containing the pieces of stationery.

"I took this on impulse. She told me these were lucky numbers. But when I started asking about her gambling habits, she became very uncomfortable. Then she shredded this right in front of me. I fished it out of her trash."

Grissom took the bag.

"The weirdness just keeps coming," he said. "We'll put it back together and see if it tells us anything interesting. What makes you think she has a gambling problem?"

"I don't know if it has anything to do with Bledsoe. Probably it doesn't. But I've seen this sort of thing before. She said she used to gamble, but when I asked how long she'd been clean, she gave me a speech about how she didn't have a problem. Never had a problem. Couldn't imagine having a problem."

"She's got a problem," Stokes said.

"My thoughts exactly," Grissom said. "You should run a background check—"

"Already done," Brass said. "No record."

"Or maybe nobody's caught her doing anything yet," Stokes said.

"Well, this is all very interesting, but unless we can develop some tangible connection between Ms. Lazaran's theoretical gambling difficulties and this case, it's beside the point," Grissom said. "What do we have that's a bit more germane to the issue?"

Brass sighed heavily and rubbed his eyes.

"Well, first and foremost, I think we're getting soft," he said. "Someone came very close to waltzing this whole mess right past us. If it hadn't been for the owner of the drywall company, we never would have compared those two reports."

"Why would we?" Vega offered. "Why would a high-profile murder in a place like Passion Lake Preserve have anything to do with some unemployed guy getting capped halfway across town?"

"Good question," Grissom said, looking at Willows.

She took the cue, producing a ballistics report and summarizing it for the group.

"We compared the slugs that killed Bledsoe with those we took out of Espinoza," she said. "They come from the same nine-millimeter pistol. The weapon hasn't been located, but Espinoza had a Glock Model 19 registered to him. It was his sidearm from when he worked as a casino security guard."

"Any physical evidence at Espinoza's place that might, in light of current developments, connect him with the Bledsoe crime?" Grissom asked. "Any trace of the stolen goods?"

"Nothing," Willows said. "Nothing except for the bling we found stuck to his chest. Dr. Robbins extracted it during the autopsy. The piece, after we bent it back into its proper shape, was found to be a simple three-quarter-karat diamond on a hook. You could buy pretty much the same thing at any mall."

"Could it be his?" Stokes asked.

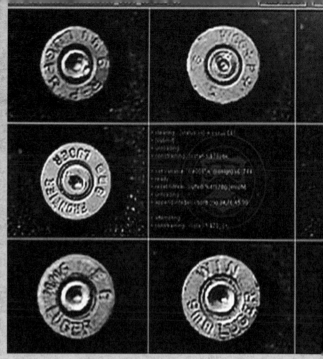

"Well, his earlobes were burned off, so there's no way to tell if he was pierced," Willows said. "However, the earring is almost certainly a woman's design. So, probably not. Judging by its position, he could have been lying on it when he died."

"We can check it against the stuff taken from the Bledsoe house," Brass offered. "For insurance purposes, they kept a careful inventory. There's photos of every piece, from multiple angles. We should be able to match the cut of the rock—if there's a match to be made."

"My gut tells me there isn't," Willows said. "Like I said, this piece could have come from any mall. It would only set you back a couple hundred bucks. Not exactly Charlotte Bledsoe's style."

"Anything else at Espinoza's place that seems helpful?" Grissom asked.

"Nothing obvious," Willows continued. "The house was scorched. But I did extract a hair sample from the shower drain."

Willows handed over the terse analyses of the drain's contents to Grissom, who scanned it, frowning. His frown grew more pronounced as he progressed down the page.

"Genetic analysis shows the drain contains hair from three different people," Willows said, paraphrasing for the rest of the group. "There's Espinoza, along with two unidentified persons. Also some sort of animal hair. Hodges is working on it, but he's pretty sure it's feline."

"A cat?" Stokes offered.

"Definitely a cat," Willows continued. "But not a housecat."

"Well, if it wasn't a housecat, then what?" Brass said. Willows sighed deeply.

"Probably more like a tiger," she said.

"A tiger," Grissom said. He put down the piece of paper

and gazed off into the middle distance.

"I don't suppose anyone saw a tiger fleeing the scene with a bag of jewelry in its mouth, did they?" Stokes asked, grinning.

Willows shot him a weary look.

"Let's set that aside for the moment," Grissom said. "Anything else interesting? What about the accelerant used to burn the place?'

"Standard commercial lighter fluid," Willows said. "We found the half-melted plastic container just inside the back door. No prints. The killer probably found it at the scene. There are traces of the same product on the charcoal grill in Espinoza's backyard. I was wondering if there was some unob-trusive way that I could check the Bledsoe house for residue."

"Good luck with that," Vega said. "Yesterday I was out at Passion Lake all day. There were two maid service vans in the Bledsoe driveway pretty much the whole time."

Willows swore under her breath.

"That's a problem for us, but it's not necessarily suspicious," Stokes offered. "Her husband bled to death on the floor. I can't imagine a better reason to do some spring cleaning."

"I suppose so," Grissom said. "But she's had a lot of people out there lately. The security company, for instance. She just had to have those cameras removed as soon as possible. There's no logical reason for that."

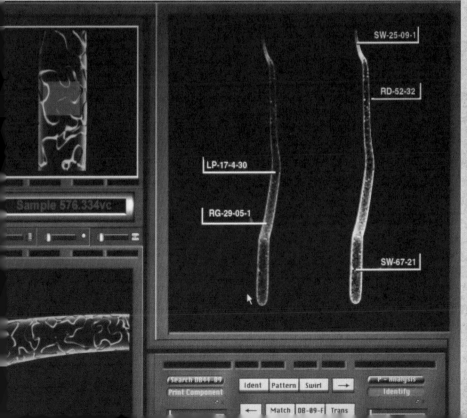

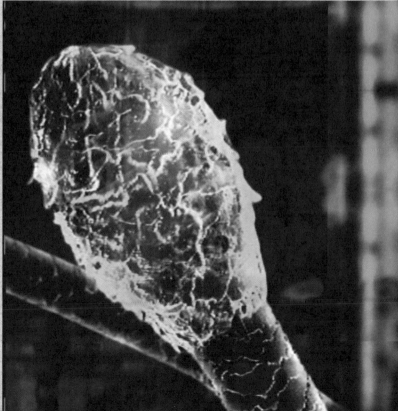

"No logical reason," Stokes said. "But it's still understandable from a certain point of view. If she really did have an affair and if her husband caught her by using video surveillance, she probably wasn't too fond of that gear. Plus, having the house wired like that is creepy."

Grissom could sense that the meeting was veering off into the weeds. There was too much conjecture based on too little information.

"I don't see how Charlotte Bledsoe could have done this," Stokes said. "The timing is too tight. But if she did do it, we'll find traces of the accelerant all over her car's interior. We might even get gun residue off the steering wheel."

Willows looked at Grissom.

"There's no way we're obtaining a search warrant for her vehicle based on this," he said. "But perhaps we don't need to. Charlotte Bledsoe calls pretty regularly, asking for updates. I'll invite her to drop by." He turned to Catherine. "Can you spare some people to go over her car?"

"What about a search warrant?"

"I'm pretty sure that after we talk, we won't need one."

"Do you want me to sit in?"

"Ordinarily yes, but in this case I'm going to try something unorthodox," Grissom said. "If it fails, I'd prefer to have as few witnesses as possible. However, I would like to ask for your help with something else. Remember how you wanted to check the Bledsoe house for signs of accelerant on the floor?"

"Of course."

"Well, you don't have to bother. We brought the rug that Mel Bledsoe died on back with us. And if I recall correctly from looking at the home surveillance tapes, Charlotte Bledsoe walked right across it."

"On my way," Willows said as she turned and vanished down the hallway.

．．．．．．．．．．．．．．．．．．．．．．．．．．．．．．．．．．．．．

Less than an hour after speaking to Grissom on the phone, Charlotte Bledsoe was back at CSI headquarters. Grissom was informed of her arrival by an officer posted in the building's garage. She was driving the silver Mercedes SL-Class Roadster that she'd left at the airport when she went on her spa trip. It was, of course, the same vehicle she'd driven home—with, perhaps, a stop en route—on the night of the murders.

Grissom, along with Brass, led her not to his office but into an interrogation room—the same one in which Kevin Williams had recently spilled his guts.

Brass noted that she betrayed no concern about the change of setting. She seemed not to grasp its significance.

"What have you learned?" she asked Grissom. "What couldn't you tell me over the phone?"

Grissom passed his right hand through his hair and adopted a studied look of unease. He was trying to do something that didn't come naturally   act as if he wasn't sure what to do next. He needed to look inside Charlotte Bledsoe's vehicle. And because he didn't have enough evidence for a warrant, he needed to talk her into volunteering.

Not an easy job.

"It's something of a personal matter," he said softly. "I thought that, considering the subject, we might want to speak in person."

"So that we can clear this up quickly, without there being any chance of . . . . unflattering publicity," Brass chimed in.

Bledsoe looked from Grissom to Brass, seemingly at a loss.

"What are you talking about?" she said.

Grissom adopted a perfectly executed sorry-to-trouble-you smile.

"During our investigation, someone stated that you were having . . . . well, I guess there's no delicate way of saying it. They said you were, uh, seeing Mateo Espinoza."

Bledsoe's expression darkened. "Who said that?"

"I'm afraid we can't reveal the source," Brass offered. "But since Espinoza died on the same night as your husband, I'm afraid we need to discuss the matter. Can you please tell us about your relationship with him? Specifically, how you met and how long you were together?"

"I don't know what you're talking about," Bledsoe spat. "I've never spoken to anyone named Espinoza."

Grissom leaned back in his chair and sighed.

"If you truly want to help this investigation," Brass said, "then you need to answer truthfully. So far this link between you and Mr. Espinoza is our only possible lead."

Bledsoe's eyes grew wide.

"Are you accusing me of being involved?" she said.

"We're not accusing you of anything," Grissom said. "We simply want to establish as many facts as possible. And your denying a relationship isn't helping. You understand what we do here, right?"

"Excuse me?" Bledsoe said.

"We go over crime scenes with a fine-tooth comb, extract-ing clues that most laymen wouldn't even realize were clues. Like, for instance, hair samples. Even though a large portion of Espinoza's house burned down, our people were still able to remove some significant hair samples. Using DNA matching, we learned that although most of it was Espinoza's, at least one of the subsets was from a woman."

"What does that prove?" Bledsoe asked.

"I won't bore you with the details of how we match these hairs to their owners. I will if you wish, but can't you spare me the trouble and just tell us what you know?"

Brass worked hard to keep from smiling. It was a daring gambit.

Bledsoe sat quietly for a long moment. In the silent room, Grissom imagined he could hear the wheels turning in her head. "All right," she said. "But you must promise me that this information doesn't get to the press."

"If it isn't relevant to the case, it won't get out," Grissom said. "Now please enlighten us."

Bledsoe sighed and then flicked something off the lapel of her jacket. She stared at the surface of the metal table in front of her. She was still staring at it when she started speaking. "I don't usually do this sort of thing," she said in a quiet mono-tone. "I'm happily married. Or, happy enough. It was several months ago. I was coming home from shopping, and as I walked in the house this man—one of the guys remodeling our basement—he gouged his hand on a nail. I offered to help him dress the wound. Did I ever mention that in my previous life—back before I married Mel—I was a nurse?"

"No," Brass said. "Please continue."

"I took him to the downstairs guest bathroom and cleaned

and bandaged his hand," Bledsoe said. "And that was how we met."

"What happened then?" Grissom said.

"Nothing, at first," Bledsoe responded. "As I said, I have a good marriage. But Mel wasn't around much, and his work made him extremely tense. So I began seeing Mateo. We would meet and talk. Then one day we—we went upstairs."

"I see," Brass said. "How long did the relationship continue?"

"I wouldn't dignify it with that term," Bledsoe responded. "We met at the house only twice. After that, maybe three times at his squalid little . . . place. Then I broke it off."

"Why?" Brass asked.

"Because it was so unseemly. I was having a relationship with a day laborer. What if someone found out?"

"Did your husband suspect?" Grissom asked.

"No," Bledsoe said. She didn't elaborate.

"I see," Grissom said. "So how did you end it?"

"I told him one day that I didn't want to see him anymore. And he didn't seem to mind. Right after that, he stopped coming around. I understand he quit his job. After that, I never saw him again."

"All right," Grissom said. "You say your husband didn't know. Would you care to reconsider that?"

Bledsoe finally looked up from the table.

"Mel didn't know," she said. "I ended the affair myself."

"Your husband never said a word about it?" Grissom asked.

"How could he?" Bledsoe said. "The man lived at his office. He didn't have eyes in the back of his head."

Brass looked at Grissom.

"Just a couple more questions. Why did you risk meeting Mr. Espinoza at your home when you knew about the security cameras?"

Bledsoe seemed genuinely nonplussed by the question.

"Why would that matter?" she said. "We never got together when Mel was actually home. I was stupid, but not that stupid."

"Yes, but with his Internet connection, he could access the cameras from his laptop," Grissom said.

"What?" Bledsoe asked.

"All he had to do was type in an access code and he could peek from anyplace," Brass explained.

A vivid spectrum of emotions burst across Bledsoe's face. They came and went as fast as summer thunderstorms. Grissom thought he saw surprise, then anger, then shame. Finally, resignation.

"He never said anything about that to me," she finally said in a quiet voice. "I never knew."

"Perhaps he did see you and Mr. Espinoza together," Brass offered. "Maybe he was waiting for the right moment to tell you."

Bledsoe's mouth formed a mirthless, tired smile.

"You don't know Mel," she said. "He didn't wait to take people on. He just wasn't wired that way. Ask anyone. If someone crossed him, he confronted them. I think that's why he's dead now. When that person broke into our home, Mel should have called the police and hidden under the bed. But he didn't. If Mel had known about me and Mateo, he wouldn't have been coy. I'd be out on the street right now."

"All right," Grissom said. "Then the only thing left to do is examine your vehicle for trace evidence."

"Evidence of what?"

"Given your relationship with Espinoza, we need to check to make sure you weren't at the crime scene. If there's nothing to be found, then this particular matter can end here."

"Fine," Bledsoe said. She produced her key and handed it to Grissom. "Which one of you is going to call me a cab?"

· · · · · · · · · · · · · · · · · · · · · · · · · ·

Hours later Grissom was sitting in Willows's office. Her desk was covered with freshly minted reports.

"We found a hairbrush in the glove compartment," she said. "The hair matches with one of the female sets from the drain. So that puts her at the house."

"Okay," Grissom said. "So we've got physical evidence for the part of the relationship she admits to. Anything else?"

"No accelerant residue, no sign of gun residue in the vehicle."

"Figures."

"According to a receipt in the glove compartment, the car was detailed yesterday. That could account for the lack of physical evidence. But we found plenty on the rug that Mel Bledsoe died on. It's covered with traces of the accelerant."

"So we have her," Grissom said. "Or at least enough to justify a search warrant of her house."

"Let's call a judge," Willows said.

· · · · · · · · · · · · · · · · · · · · · · · · · ·

When the CSIs returned to the Bledsoe home, they did so in force—three black SUVs plus two marked cars from the regular LVPD. They didn't expect trouble; there was just a lot of territory to cover.

"I'm beginning to hate this place," Stokes said as he hopped out of his vehicle, field kit in hand.

Willows patted him on the back. "That's the spirit. You can hand Mrs. Bledsoe the search warrant."

The expedition fulfilled all expectations. Charlotte Bledsoe was apoplectic. She made a phone call, and almost immediately a grim-faced attorney in a very expensive suit materialized at her side. As the CSIs combed the house, the two stood in a corner, whispering back and forth.

Willows and Stokes paid particular attention to the home's

entryway and living room, checking for accelerant residue and, just perhaps, traces of gun oil or powder on surfaces that might have been touched. But it was obvious that the cleaning crew Bledsoe had hired had done an extremely thorough job.

Upstairs, Grissom examined the master suite and Mel Bledsoe's adjoining home office.

He was sitting at Bledsoe's desk when Brass walked in.

"Find anything?" Brass asked.

"No," he said absently. "And it bothers me. You said Drew Lazaran mentioned Bledsoe using a laptop to monitor the house. Did anyone recover one from his office?"

"No," Brass said. "There wasn't one."

"And there's nothing here," Grissom said. "So either Mrs. Bledsoe did something with it, or perhaps it was stolen in the robbery."

The two took the matter to a decidedly uncooperative Charlotte Bledsoe. Still fuming in the downstairs entryway, she was trying without success to reduce Catherine Willows to ashes by glaring at her.

"This is unconscionable," she said to Grissom.

"I have a question about your husband's laptop computer," Grissom replied. "Where might we find it?"

Bledsoe's lawyer whispered something in her ear.

"I wouldn't know," she said. "If it isn't here, then I assume it's at the office."

"Did he leave it there often?" Grissom asked.

Bledsoe thought for a moment.

"No," she said. "No, he didn't. As a matter of fact, he almost always had it with him. Especially lately. He even went so far as to lock it in the upstairs safe at night."

A thorough search of the home's every nook and cranny turned up nothing of obvious use—and no laptop. By late afternoon, the team was ready to call it a day.

"All right," Grissom said during the ride back. "What have we got?"

Brass drove the SUV while Grissom rode shotgun. Stokes and Willows sat dejectedly in the backseat.

"Very little," Willows said. "The entryway and living room are squeaky clean. There are tests to run, but if they turn up anything useful, I'll be very surprised."

"Same here," Stokes said. "Whenever I need to clean my McMansion, I'll definitely hire the people she used."

"I'm worried about the laptop," Grissom said.

"Espinoza might have grabbed it on the way out," Brass said. "It's light, and it would be a lot easier to sell than the jewelry. Maybe he saw it on the desk and scooped it up."

"Maybe," Grissom said. "But there was also an iPod on the desk too. If he was going to get grabby, why not take that? Why bother with a computer?"

"All after he'd just murdered someone," Brass said.

"Maybe there was something on the computer that he—or someone else—wanted," Stokes said. "Maybe that's what he really came for."

It was something to think about. But, as usual, too much information-free conjecture bothered Grissom.

"Interesting idea," he said. "But let's concentrate on what we've got. We know Charlotte Bledsoe had an affair with Espinoza. We know Espinoza and Mel Bledsoe were killed with the same weapon. We know that Charlotte Bledsoe—or someone—tracked traces of the accelerant used to burn down

Espinoza's house all over the rug upon which Mel died."

"And that's pretty much it," Brass said. "Not enough to make a strong case."

"Plus there are the other questions," Stokes said.

"Which are?" Grissom asked.

"First and foremost, what does a tiger have to do with any of this?"

Grissom, Brass, and Willows laughed.

"And why was Mel always reading haiku?"

Brass and Willows laughed again. Grissom didn't. Instead, a thoughtful look crossed his face.

"I'd like to take a look at that little book again," he said.

. . . . . . . . . . . . . . . . . . . . . . . . . . . . . .

**B**ack at the office, Grissom put on a pair of gloves and carefully examined the blood-spattered book of haiku. He was looking at—and for—nothing in particular.

Grissom tried to divine what a person like Bledsoe saw in such spare, contemplative words. Handwritten notes in the margins suggested that Bledsoe had assigned months to twelve of the haiku—but why? Grissom recognized the August poem as one of the most famous and enigmatic haiku of all time. Its author was a seventeenth-century master named Matsuo Bashō.

*Old pond / a frog jumps / the sound of water*

Grissom parsed through the words. As he did so, he found his own mood changing. Thinking about the old pond, the frog,

and the water seemed to help him focus. Some of the day's stress fell away.

He took a moment and leafed through some of the other works. Perhaps, just perhaps, Bledsoe kept this book around because it helped him to focus.

Surely there were stranger things than a man beset by troubles on every side taking solace from the written word.

Except . . . Grissom just didn't buy it.

He closed the book, returned it to its evidence bag, and pulled off his gloves. Then, on impulse, he sat back in his chair and closed his eyes.

The sounds of the busy office receded. Grissom imagined a pond. Imagined the sound of water. Imagined a frog jumping and disrupting the still, mirrorlike surface. He thought about how that one tiny event could alter the shape of the entire body of water.

Just as one new fact—or one old, ignored fact seen from a different perspective—could alter an entire case.

Grissom sat up and opened his eyes. The chaotic world returned. He picked up his phone and called Brass.

"I just had an idea," he said.

# CRIME SCENE DO NOT CROSS

# CRIME SCENE
## DO NOT
# CROSS

It's time to put your detective skills to the test. Before turning the page, use the evidence recovered throughout the investigation to answer the following questions: Who killed Melvin Bledsoe—and why? Who killed Mateo Espinoza—and why? What is the significance of the haiku book? And why was tiger hair recovered at the crime scene?

Drew Lazaran honored Grissom's **request** to meet at her apartment, though she was **curious** as to **why.**

"I WANTED TO BRING YOU up-to-date on the case," Grissom said when he arrived at her door the next morning. "I thought that meeting someplace other than the office would be less distracting."

"Of course," Lazaran said. "Please, come in."

The living room's decor was consciously kitschy, right down to the big glass ashtrays and an amoeba-shaped coffee table.

"Quite an interesting theme you've got here," Grissom said.

"I call it Vintage Vegas," Lazaran said. "I bought most of this stuff at estate auctions. Also eBay. May I take your coat?"

Grissom surrendered his jacket. When Lazaran opened her closet door, he noticed a purse on the shelf. It was strangely familiar to him.

"That's unusual," he said. "Is it real?"

"I honestly don't know. I bought it for the kitsch appeal. Don't really use it much anymore."

They walked together into Lazaran's smallish home office. She sat down behind the desk while Grissom took a chair in front. Which told him a great deal. Rather than confront him face-to-face, she wanted something between them. Grissom was happy to let her feel a false sense of security. He already knew far more about her than she realized.

"As you probably learned from the news, Charlotte Bledsoe is now our primary suspect," he said. "She had a sexual relationship with Mateo Espinoza. What isn't generally known is that we found traces of the accelerant used to burn Espinoza's house on a rug in the Bledsoe home."

"I see," Lazaran said. "So you think she used Espinoza to rob the house, then killed him?"

"Well, there's plenty of evidence that points in Mrs. Bledsoe's direction, but I'm not satisfied that we have a solid case."

"You don't have enough to go to trial?"

"Oh, we could go to trial. We'd probably even win. I'm just not convinced we have the right person."

Lazaran seemed to stiffen a bit.

"Why is that?" she said.

"We took a hair sample at Espinoza's home. It contained hair from two women. One was Charlotte Bledsoe. The other is unidentified. It's red, but that's about all we can say at this point. I'd like to know who that second individual is."

"Do you have any leads?"

"Not a one. But that's not your worry, because you couldn't possibly have anything to offer on that account. You didn't know Mr. Espinoza, correct?"

"That's right," Lazaran said.

"I want to ask you about something else. Mr. Bledsoe's laptop computer is missing. We believe it was stolen from his home, right along with the jewelry. However, we're not sure why Espinoza would have bothered. You knew Mr. Bledsoe as well as anyone. Did he keep anything on his computer that would be of interest to an outside party?"

"Not that I know of," Lazaran said.

"I ask because you knew about the alleged affair between Charlotte Bledsoe and Mateo Espinoza."

"There's nothing 'alleged' about it. I only found out because I was in the right place at the right time."

"So, Mr. Bledsoe never mentioned anything else that was bothering him? Anything that he might have stored on his computer?"

"I wouldn't know what kinds of files he had. They were password protected, and he went to great lengths to protect that password."

"Because he was a very private person," Grissom said.

"Yes. But also careful. I'm sure he must have written it down someplace. He would never have solely trusted his memory with something that important."

"I see," Grissom said. He leaned forward in his chair. "Would you like to hear my pet theory?"

"Of course," Lazaran said uncertainly.

"In the scenario that we—well, I suppose it really was you—put forth, Charlotte Bledsoe was caught by her husband, on camera, having sex with her lover. Mel Bledsoe wanted to divorce. That meant Charlotte Bledsoe, thanks to their unforgiving prenup, would have to abandon the lifestyle to which she'd grown accustomed. So she convinced her boy toy to break into the house while she was away, kill her husband, then steal her jewelry to make it look like a robbery gone bad. With me so far?"

"Yes. Please go on."

"To cover her tracks, once she got back into town she stopped at Espinoza's place, killed him, and torched the house. Then she drove home and acted the part of the newly bereaved widow."

"Well that sounds . . . plausible," Lazaran said.

"Ah, but it doesn't sound plausible. I can tell by the tone of your voice that *you* don't even buy it, and you're the one who put it forward. The timing of her arrival at the airport and the Espinoza killing is just too tight. Maybe a professional could have pulled it off, but not a socialite on her way back from a spa retreat. Plus, my gut tells me that while Mrs. Bledsoe can indeed be an overbearing, elitist pain in the ass, she's not a killer."

Grissom leaned forward, closing the distance between him and Lazaran.

"But here's what really concerns me," he said, almost whispering. "If Charlotte Bledsoe killed Espinoza and then burned down the house, there should be traces of accelerant on her shoes. But when we checked them, we didn't find any."

"Maybe she wiped it off," Lazaran said.

"That's a possibility, but not likely. She wore very expensive Italian-made pumps. With a very fine finish—the kind you wouldn't wear in the rain. If she tried to wipe them down, the damage would be obvious. Plus, even if she wiped the shoes, there would still be enough residue left behind for us to detect."

"Perhaps she changed shoes. The woman has plenty. I've seen her closet."

"That's what I thought at first. Change shoes and you don't have to worry about the residue. There's just one problem. You know the big rug in the living room? The one Mel Bledsoe died on? We have video of her walking across it several times on the night of the killing. And there is residue on the rug that matches perfectly with what we found at the other crime scene. Clearly someone left it there. But who?"

Lazaran looked as if she was about to combust. With a supreme effort, she spoke.

"Who, indeed?" she said.

"Well, Mrs. Bledsoe would have picked up a bit of the accelerant if she'd walked on the rug after someone else deposited it, so we know it wasn't there before her arrival. As for the people who came later, none of them visited the Espinoza crime scene first."

"Are you sure?" Lazaran said.

"Very sure. We checked. Well, we checked everyone but you. Which is how you can really help me with this case. The shoes you were wearing that night—do you still have them?"

"I don't remember what I wore. It was a very stressful evening."

"Yes, it was," Grissom said. "A very stressful night. Does this help?"

He pulled out a screen grab from the Bledsoe's security tape. It showed Lazaran wearing a pair of tan heels.

She picked up the photo. It wavered in her hand just slightly as she studied it.

"I'm afraid I don't have these anymore," she finally said. "That very evening I broke one of the heels. I'm afraid they're out at the landfill by now."

"I see," Grissom said. "Would you mind if we looked in your closet?"

"I'm afraid I would mind. I would consider that an invasion of privacy."

"That's fine. I'll go sit in my car and phone in a request for a search warrant. When it's granted—which should take about ten minutes—I'll return with several LVPD officers. We will search this place from top to bottom, and perhaps, if we're lucky, we'll find the missing jewelry and the murder weapon and maybe the laptop, too. But you know what we'll certainly do, Ms. Lazaran? We will take your shoes. Every single pair. Even your special goin' murderin' shoes, which I'm guessing aren't at the landfill, but are still parked in your closet."

Lazaran sat back in her chair. Something about her face changed. The tension bled away. She'd made a decision.

"A person in my situation can't go to prison. If I land in

DREW LAZARAN // 12:41AM

there I'm as good as dead. I'm sorry, Mr. Grissom."

Lazaran pulled out a pistol. Grissom stiffened in his chair. He recognized it as a Glock Model 19—the same weapon used to kill both Bledsoe and Espinoza.

"I think I'm going to run away," she said. "And I can't have you chasing me."

Grissom swallowed hard.

"You don't want to kill a cop," he said. "Then you'll be in real trouble."

"I didn't want to kill anybody," she said. "And I'm already in real trouble. More than you know."

She leveled the weapon on Grissom's chest.

. . . . . . . . . . . . . . . . . . . . . . . . . . . . . . . .

Twenty minutes earlier and many miles away, specialist AV technician Archie Johnson also cracked the Bledsoe case, though by a different route.

Before leaving to see Lazaran, Grissom had stopped by and asked for a close-up shot of, of all things, the woman's shoes. Johnson complied, grabbing a grainy-but-serviceable image that was taken as Lazaran loitered in the Bledsoes' living room.

The seemingly nonsensical request got him thinking once more about the surveillance footage salvaged from the home's monitoring system.

Which led him, for the umpteenth time, to watch it.

It seemed like a fool's errand. There was nothing to see. Yet for some reason he kept looking, even though his eyes hurt, just like when he sat too close to the screen at the movies.

A part of his brain seemed to think there was something there. It was screaming at the conscious portion to notice.

First, there was seemingly endless footage of Bledsoe dead on the floor. If you watched closely—and Johnson watched very closely, indeed—you could actually see the blood stain on the rug slowly darken as the victim's body emptied out.

Then the cops arrived. Johnson recognized one of the first responders from a couple of crime scenes he'd visited in person. The two disappeared off-screen, weapons drawn, doubtlessly going from room to room, looking for the shooter.

Then, a while later, came more cops—Brass among them. Next Charlotte Bledsoe, looking distraught at the sight of her husband on the floor. Next Drew Lazaran, looking only slightly less frazzled and out of sorts. She

came in and looked around. Then she conferred for several minutes with Brass. Then she looked around again and left.

Suddenly Johnson sat bolt upright, his eyes riveted to the screen. He'd spotted something. Just to be sure, he toggled the image back and forth several times, making sure his eyes hadn't deceived him.

He'd finally received the message his subconscious mind wanted him to have.

Johnson ran down the hall to Brass's office.

"Where's Grissom?" he said.

"Talking to Drew Lazaran for the Bledsoe case," Brass said. "Why?"

"You've got to get out there," he said. "She killed Espinoza."

• • • • • • • • • • • • • • • • • • • • • • • • • •

Lazaran and Grissom both heard sirens in the distance. As they grew louder, the woman's hands began to shake.

Grissom had no idea where the sirens were headed. But it was a chance—maybe his one chance—to save his life.

"It's over," he said. "Even if you shoot me, you won't get far. Just put the weapon down and we can both walk out of here alive."

Lazaran shook her head. She kept the gun leveled at Grissom's chest.

"No," she said. "I'm not going to prison. I'd rather die."

The sirens kept growing louder. Perhaps they really were coming to Grissom's rescue.

"His computer's in my desk," Lazaran said. "It will explain everything. But I won't tell you how to access it. Bledsoe's laptop is password protected, and I'm the only one who knows the code. So, good luck."

She placed the barrel of the gun against her right temple.

"I wouldn't do it that way," Grissom said, sensing there might still be time—and a way—to dissuade her.

"Excuse me?" Lazaran said.

"If you shoot from the side like that, it may not be fatal. I've seen plenty of failed gun suicides where the shooter flinched at the last moment or the concussion from the pistol altered the bullet's trajectory. They blew off their faces—nose, eyes, mouth—but missed their brains. They didn't die."

Lazaran simply stared at him, the weapon still pointed at her head.

"If you want to do it right, I'd advise firing through the chin, straight up into the skull," Grissom continued. "Though there's still the possibility of blowing your face off rather than your brains out. Ideally, you should get a mouthful of water and hold it while you fire. The liquid magnifies the force of the concussion. It will spray your brain all over the wall behind you."

"I don't have any water," Lazaran said.

"Just as well. Going out like this is an ugly way to die. And, to be frank, you don't seem like the type. You feel like a survivor to me."

"I am."

"Then give me the weapon. You don't want to have it when my friends arrive. It will just make more trouble."

Lazaran pulled the gun away from her head. She looked at it for a moment, then tossed it onto the desk. Grissom reached out and swept it away in one smooth motion.

"I really didn't want it to work out this way," Lazaran said forlornly. "If things had gone as I'd wanted, no one would have gotten hurt."

"I know," Grissom said. "I hear that all the time."

• • • • • • • • • • • • • • • • • • • • • • • • • • •

At that instant, he heard the front door give way, followed by Brass's voice. The LVPD had arrived. The cops swept rapidly from room to room. Grissom kept his chair, identified himself, and gave his location.

Brass, gun in hand, appeared at the door. He found Grissom on his feet and Lazaran still behind her desk, her face in her hands.

"It's okay," Grissom said. "You need to take her into custody for—"

"For the murders of Mel Bledsoe and Mateo Espinoza," Brass said. "We know."

"Seriously?" Grissom asked. "How do you know?"

"Archie spotted something on the surveillance video. Something we'd overlooked half a dozen times. How did *you* figure it out?"

"I suspected. I didn't actually know until I saw the inside of her coat closet."

"I didn't bother to check my wrap. What did you find?"

Two uniformed officers entered the room and took charge of Lazaran. Grissom got up and, on unsteady legs, walked back to the living room. He opened the closet door and pointed to a small purse hanging on a peg.

"Bull's-eye," Brass said. "That's our kitty."

The purse was covered in authentic tiger hide.

"She's big into retro Vegas stuff," Grissom said. "Probably got this secondhand someplace. She didn't know it was real, but it is. And just like fur of a regular housecat, it sheds. Every time she went to Espinoza's place with that thing under her arm, she left a little bit of it behind. Just enough to get her caught."

"How did she know him?" Brass asked.

"I'm not too clear on that, but I think she'll enlighten us

later," Grissom said. "Right now I'd like to take a look at Bledsoe's computer. And to do that, we need to refer to his haiku book."

"You really think this is the time to read poetry?" Brass asked.

"Of course not. He was using the book to keep track of his computer passwords. Right in plain sight."

"How did Lazaran get it, and what did she want it for?"

"I have a theory. I'll see if it's correct when we interrogate her."

A uniform brought the laptop computer, found in the second drawer of Lazaran's desk, into the living room and handed it to Grissom. He set it down on the room's amoeba-shaped coffee table and turned it on.

"Battery looks good," he said. "Let's see what happens."

Instead of a menu, a request for an access code popped up, along with a box with a blinking cursor inside.

"I'll bet this thing uses a serious encryption program," Grissom said. "If I've got this wrong, we may never get at the files. But I don't think I have it wrong."

He typed in opafjtsow16441694.

"What the hell is that?" Brass said.

"It was written on the stationery Lazaran shredded. Something that I'm sure she got rid of to cover her tracks. It's also, by the way, the first letter of each word of a haiku in Bledsoe's poetry book, plus the years of the author's birth and death."

Grissom pressed Enter.

"We're in," he said.

The computer opened to a file directory. The files read "Embezzlor01," "Embezzlor02" and "Embezzlor03."

"Jackpot," Grissom said.

As the apartment filled with more and more emergency responders, the two men bent over the screen and read.

Hours later Grissom and Brass sat down with Lazaran in an interrogation room. Only this time, instead of being dressed in a kitschy thrift store ensemble, she wore a baggy jail uniform.

"Have any trouble getting into Mr. Bledsoe's computer?" she asked tonelessly.

"Nope," Grissom said. "Figured it out on our own."

"Is there any way I can assist? Something that might shave a few years off my sentence? I'd love to get out before midcentury, if that's possible."

"We'll see," Brass said. "Right now, the most helpful thing you can do is answer our questions truthfully and thoroughly."

"I want to say up-front that I didn't want to hurt anybody. I was responsible for a lot of things, but not for the murders. I mean, I guess I was responsible for the second one, but I had no choice. And I don't hold malice toward anyone involved. Except for Mateo, who was an idiot. Really, just an idiot."

"Please start from the beginning," Brass said.

Lazaran sighed. She looked first at Grissom, then at Brass. "I started working at Bledsoe Homes five years ago," she said. "This was during the good times—both for the housing market and for me. Bledsoe was making deals left and right. People called him a high roller, but they had no idea. I was the real high roller. I gambled a lot, and I lost a lot. Far more than I could afford to lose."

"Ah," Brass said. "How much were you in the hole for?"

"About $460,000," Lazaran said. "Toward the end, I took out some loans from some very bad people. The kind of people who want their cash back, no matter what. So, to stave them off I started draining funds from Bledsoe Homes. First a little, then more and more.

"No one seemed to suspect because, at the time, there was plenty coming in. But things started to change when the market went south. Everyone pinched pennies, which made stealing them harder. I remember Bledsoe occasionally saying that he didn't like how the books looked—and promising that he was going to investigate. I knew from experience that when he decided to 'look into' something, he wouldn't stop until he found what he wanted. So I decided to act preemptively and neutralize him before he neutralized me."

"Kill him?" Grissom asked.

"No," Lazaran said, with some heat. "By 'neutralize,' I don't mean kill. I didn't plan to kill anyone. I didn't need to. You see, Mr. Bledsoe and I had a special relationship. I knew things about him. There was a lot more to my job than anyone—even Mrs. Bledsoe—realized."

"I see," Brass said. "So you were also his . . . "

"You don't see anything," Lazaran said. "I wasn't his mistress. We never had a sexual relationship. In some ways it was far more intimate than that. A man in Mr. Bledsoe's position—a man with his temperament—doesn't like to show weakness. Not to others, not to himself. But he had one, and it was a doozy."

In an uncharacteristic show of emotion, Grissom smacked his forehead with his right hand and smiled.

"Dyscalculia," he said.

"Wow," Lazaran replied, genuinely impressed. "You're good."

"Excuse me?" Brass said.

"Bledsoe suffered from dyscalculia," Grissom continued. "It's like dyslexia, except with numbers. That's why he didn't arm his security system. He could never remember the code sequence. It's why he hid the access code to his laptop in that haiku book. It was highly sensitive information, but he had to write it down somewhere because he couldn't memorize it."

"Actually, I think he had a mild form of dyslexia along with a more severe type of dyscalculia," Lazaran offered. "That's why he hired me, with my accounting degree, to be his 'administrative assistant.' Let's just say I didn't spend much time writing letters or circulating memos. I helped him decipher spreadsheets and financial reports."

"You knew everything," Brass said.

"Absolutely everything," Lazaran continued. "It was an unbelievable opportunity for someone in my circumstances. He knew someone was skimming from him, but I was in the perfect position to steer him away from the truth. But I also understood that—in his slow, plodding way—he was looking at the numbers himself, in private. It must have been supremely difficult, but he had huge reserves of will. I knew that eventually he would figure it out.

"So, like I said, I tried to neutralize him. I started with spying. I knew that Bledsoe had Internet access to that crazy Orwellian camera system in his house. I decided I wanted it, too. Of course, I knew he must have written down his computer access code somewhere. It took me a while to realize it was hidden in plain sight."

"The haiku book," Brass said.

"Exactly. One day he just showed up with it. I'd see him looking through it at odd times—always, I noticed, just before he logged onto his top-secret laptop. He used to brag that its encryption software exceeded 'CIA standards,' whatever that means. Maybe so, but his password storage method was purely bronze age."

Grissom glanced over at Brass.

"One day I walked around his desk while he was logging on, and got a fleeting glimpse of the password before he hit Enter," Lazaran continued. "I saw a long string of letters ending with the digits 1694. And that damn haiku book was open, face-down, to a specific page. At just that moment one of the senior sales reps asked if Bledsoe could step into the conference room. As soon as he was gone, I grabbed the book. The code was a lot simpler than Bledsoe led on. All he did was assign months to twelve of the poems. His password for any particular month became the first letter of every word in its poem, plus the years at the end. So I grabbed some stationery and wrote down all of the passwords. It worked perfectly. So now I had access to the laptop, which meant I also had access to the home monitoring system. Whenever the opportunity presented itself, I would go into Bledsoe's office, log on, and snoop."

"And, one day, you caught Charlotte Bledsoe and Mateo Espinoza doing the horizontal mambo," Brass said.

"Exactly. I recognized Mateo from his days at the Lucky Stakes—one of my favorite gambling spots. Our first meeting was pretty memorable. I left my purse at a slot machine, and he stole my wallet. Of course, he was caught instantly. Casinos have cameras everywhere but the powder rooms. I didn't want to attract attention, so I didn't press charges. But he was fired anyway. After that we struck up a relationship. He was grateful that I didn't send him to jail, and I was impressed by his looks.

But I broke it off after a couple of months. The man had no brains and no judgment. I didn't talk to him again until things got desperate."

"How's that?" Grissom prompted.

Lazaran glanced at the door, then at the ceiling. "Bledsoe started looking at me funny," she continued. "He was on to me. I knew he must be spending long evenings at home, poring over company records. He was looking for the smoking gun that would implicate the embezzler.

"It was only a matter of time. So I got in touch with Mateo. I made an excuse to run into him, and we started seeing each other again. But I made sure he never set foot at my place— or even knew where my place was. We'd have sex at his pathetic dump, and I told him about my troubles with Bledsoe. Not the truth, of course, but a version of the truth. I said that the old man wanted me to sleep with him, and that if I didn't he was going to trump up some embezzling charges and try to get me thrown in jail."

"That's a pretty sorry version of the truth," Brass said.

"It was good enough to convince poor Mateo," Lazaran said. "I think it ignited some latent, chivalrous impulse in that 60-watt brain of his. He asked what he could do to help. And when he did, I was ready with an answer."

"Kill your boss?" Grissom said.

"No. 'Kill' never entered into it. Bledsoe was paranoid about security and always played things close to the vest. He kept all his embezzling investigation materials on his laptop, and only on his laptop. If that machine were to disappear— especially in a situation that looked like a generic robbery—it would set him back months. Plus, I knew him well enough to

realize that if he perceived that his sacred home had been violated, his rage would derail his investigation indefinitely. That would buy me time to siphon off enough cash to pay my debts, then graciously leave town. Or at least that was the plan.

"I waited for a weekend I knew both of the Bledsoes would be out of town. I told Mateo to break into the house via the downstairs utility room window, which I knew, thanks to all those cameras, was unlocked. I assumed the security system would be disarmed. All Mateo had to do was sprint up the stairs, open the safe using the combination I'd already stolen, then run. With luck, we'd be gone well before the police could respond."

"But you didn't have any luck," Grissom said. "Not one bit."

"Nope," Lazaran said. "Things started going bad immediately. That evening I dressed Mateo in black shoes, black pants, a black shirt, and a black ski mask I'd bought at a thrift store. He looked like a redneck ninja. I drove him, in his car, to a stretch of perimeter nearest the Bledsoe house and cut him loose. I gave him strict instructions: Steal the computer and nothing else.

"But he was high as a kite. Don't know what he took, but it made it impossible for him to focus. He also stuffed his pistol in his pants. Because when you're robbing an empty house, you really, really need to take a gun."

"You could have called it off," Grissom pointed out.

"I should have. Instead, I drove to Passion Lake Preserve, parked in a secluded spot, and pushed him out of the car. He walked across the dark ground to the perimeter wall, then pulled out a length of rope with this three-pronged hook thing on the end that I'd bought at a camping store. He threw it over the wall. He was a very athletic man, but it took him a really extraordinary amount of time to climb that rope. Once he got up there, he reeled in the line and jumped down the other side. After that, all I could do was wait."

"How long?" Brass said.

"It was maybe fifteen minutes before he flopped back over the wall. When he finally made it back to the car, gasping for air and incoherent, I could already hear police sirens in the distance. I knew something had gone horribly wrong.

"I had to piece together what happened from Mateo's idiotic ramblings. He got to the house all right, but the window I told him to use was locked. So he broke it and crawled in. He was walking through the living room when Mr. Bledsoe suddenly appeared. And so Mateo, with perfect logic, pulled out his pistol and shot him. Repeatedly.

"But then, somehow, he kept his act together long enough to go upstairs to the bedroom. The computer was already out and sitting on Bledsoe's desk, and the safe was standing open. And in that safe Mateo saw jewelry storage boxes. He said he couldn't help himself. He stuffed everything into one bag, then grabbed the computer and left."

"What did he plan to do with the jewelry?" Brass asked.

"Who the hell knows?" Lazaran said. "That was the least of my problems. This was supposed to be quiet. If done right, no one but Bledsoe would have known there had even been a robbery. But now he was dead. And the idiot who did it was sitting next to me in the car, jabbering away. He wanted to sell the jewelry, he said. He knew a guy. We'd be rich. Blah, blah, blah. As I listened, my heart sank. I figured I might find a way to protect us from the cops, but there was no way I could pro-

tect Mateo from himself."

"So it was time to cut your losses," Grissom said.

"I guess you could put it that way," Lazaran said. "We went back to his place. Mateo, in spite of what had happened, was in a celebratory mood. He wanted a beer. I got him one. He wanted to make love. We did. Afterward, the drugs and the adrenaline that had turned him manic seemed to release their grip. I left him sleeping on his belly in his bed. I got dressed and walked back into the living room, where he'd dropped his gun on the couch. I picked it up and walked back into the bedroom. Mateo hadn't moved an inch. I put the gun about six inches from his skull and fired once. And that was all for him.

"I spent the next fifteen minutes wiping down everything I thought I'd touched. From under the kitchen sink I brought out a jug of lighter fluid he used to light his grill. I hosed down the bedroom with it, then spread a little around the public areas as well. Then I gathered up the jewelry, the gun, and the laptop, tossed a single kitchen match in the bedroom, and drove away."

"When did you hear from the LVPD?" Brass asked.

"I was maybe ten miles down the road when my cell phone rang. And when I realized it was a cop, I almost wrecked. But I managed to hold it together. The guy wanted a contact number for Charlotte, which I was able to supply on the spot."

"Why in hell did you come by their house?" Brass said.

"I wanted to see what had happened—and what you people knew. I was able to talk my way past the security gate, probably because the rent-a-cops were all freaking out. The place was crawling with cops, and news trucks were already pulling up. I realized pretty quickly that being there was a mistake. I walked in, looked around briefly, saw Mr. Bledsoe dead on the floor. I don't think it was real to me until that moment. I guess I sort of hoped against hope that Mateo got it wrong. But he didn't. So I talked to you for a couple of minutes, and then I got the hell out of there."

"So then you went home and sat tight," Brass said.

"Right," Lazaran replied. "When you turned up at my office, asking about Mateo, I played dumb. But then I remembered seeing him and Charlotte Bledsoe having sex at the house, and an idea occurred to me. I said that Mr. Bledsoe had told me he saw them together."

"So he never knew about the affair?" Grissom asked.

"Hell, no," Lazaran replied. "If he'd seen what I saw, he would have grabbed a machete and headed straight for home. The real reason he didn't go away was because he wanted to work on finding the embezzler. Finding me. I learned just how close he'd gotten when I started rooting through the files on his laptop.

"Anyway, that's the story. If I hadn't walked around on that rug, I guess you'd still be looking for the killer. Or maybe Charlotte Bledsoe would be sitting here instead of me."

"Walking around on the rug wasn't your only mistake," Grissom told her. "You also managed to lose an earring."

Lazaran's eyes grew wide.

"Damn it," she said. "I was worried about that."

"Would you like to tell us how it came to be embedded in the chest of Mr. Espinoza's severely burned body?"

Lazaran shrugged. "I guess he was lying on it when I killed him. After I got home, I noticed that my left earring had fallen out. I figured that, even if you found it, there would be no way to trace it back to me."

"You were almost right," Grissom said. "Almost."

• • • • • • • • • • • • • • • • • • • • • • • • • • • • • •

After Lazaran was led back to her cell, Grissom returned to his office and gathered his things for a quick departure. Something about having a gun pointed at him made him want to get as far from work as possible. If only for a while.

He ran into Catherine Willows on the way out.

"I really appreciate your help," he offered.

"No problem," Willows said. "By the way, you shouldn't interview suspected murderers without taking along some backup."

"Noted," Grissom replied. "I owe Archie a lot. He was staring at that useless video footage from the Bledsoe house. The one that doesn't show the robbery or the shooting or anything helpful. Except there was something helpful. Archie was looking at the footage of Drew Lazaran when he noticed she was short an earring."

"We all overlooked it," Willows said. "It was the mate to the one found on Espinoza's chest. It probably came off when they were in bed, and he wound up lying on it. When the place burned, it adhered to his chest."

"That's the theory," Grissom said. "It was literally staring us in the face. But we just couldn't see it."

He thought for a minute. Or, rather, contemplated.

"Then again, maybe Archie did notice that clue," Grissom continued. "Or a part of him did. Why else would he keep looking at that video, long after we'd decided it was irrelevant?

DREW LAZARAN // 12:40AM

DREW LAZARAN // 12:43AM

And, come to think of it, maybe I noticed, too, on some subconscious level. Maybe that's why I just couldn't accept the Bledsoe-killed-her-husband story. Maybe that's why I wanted to see Lazaran face-to-face."

"I guess the lesson is, don't trust appearances," Willows offered.

"That would have been a good lesson for Mel Bledsoe, too," Grissom said. "He built a wall around his home, hired his own private army of pretend police, hung up more spy cameras than they probably had in all of East Germany, and look what it got him."

"Three in the chest."

Grissom sighed. "At least this case introduced us to the wonderful world of haiku."

"I'd have trouble summing up this mess in seventeen syllables."

"Not me," Grissom said. "How about, 'Rich guys are so weird / don't trust their taste in poems / or women either.'"

Willows smiled.

"Now that's what I call poetic justice," she said.